THINK LIKE AN ATTORNEY

THINK LIKE AN ATTORNEY

Power Thinking for the Courtroom of Life

Brendan J. Cody, Esq.

PARALAW PUBLISHING

Think Like an Attorney © copyright 2018 by Brendan J. Cody. All rights reserved. No part of this book may be reproduced in any form whatsoever, by photography or xerography or by any other means, by broadcast or transmission, by translation into any kind of language, nor by recording electronically or otherwise, without permission in writing from the author, except by a reviewer, who may quote brief passages in critical articles or reviews.

ISBNs: 978-1-7328320-0-8 (paperback); 978-1-7328320-1-5 (ePub); 978-1-7328320-2-2 (Kindle)

Library of Congress Catalog Number: 2018911640
Printed in the United States of America
Second Printing: 2019
23 22 21 20 19 5 4 3 2

Cover design and book design by Mayfly Design

Paralaw Publishing
375 Jackson St., Ste 700W
St. Paul, MN 55101
paralawpublishing.com

To order, visit thinklikeanattorney.com or call (651) 222-7451.
Reseller discounts available.

For Bridget

Contents

Acknowledgments . . . . . *xi*

Introduction *1*

Chapter 1 . . . . . **7**

Law Student Thinking 7

Contract Law 13

Black Letter Law 22

Chapter 2 . . . . . **23**

Rookie Attorney Thinking 23

Seven Deadly Sins of the Rookie Attorney That We All Can Learn From 27

The Partner Memo 28

Deposition Skills 32

Ten Self-Protection Skills for Rookie Lawyers and You, Too 35

Black Letter Law 38

Chapter 3 . . . . . **41**

Trial Attorney Thinking 41

The Courtroom 41

The Jury Big Brain 43
Burdens of Proof 49
Evidentiary Standards 52
Rule 401. Definition of Relevant Evidence 53
Causation 54
Hearsay 56
Direct Evidence and Circumstantial Evidence . . 57
Negligence 58
Facts, Opinions, Predictions and Persuasions . . 61
Hypothetical Questions 62
Black Letter Law 64

Chapter 4 67

Veteran Attorney Thinking 67
a. Negotiation Skills 68
b. Time Management Skills 70
c. Analytical Skills: The Duty to Read 72
d. Verbal and Nonverbal Communication Skills . 76
e. Persuasive Skills/ Direct and Cross
Examination Skills 78
f. On Your Feet Thinking Skills 81
g. People Skills 83
h. Research Skills 86
i. Problem-Solving Skills 89

j. Absorption and Retention Skills 91

k. Advocacy Skills and the 4C's 92

Black Letter Law 94

Chapter 5 95

Ethical Attorney Thinking 95

Professional Aspirations 96

Rules of Professional Conduct 100

Judicial Rules of Conduct 103

Black Letter Law 105

Conclusion 107

About the Author 111

Bibliography 113

Acknowledgments

I am indebted to the many individuals who helped make this book possible. I personally wish to thank the following people: Brenda Fake, Josh Stokka, Pete Ballion, Peter Gillen, Ron Larsen, Tom Healy, Beth Brust, Tammy Ward, Pamela Kalthoff, Britta Johnson, Conor O'Neill, Vickie Carcaise, Mary Ellen Briel, Kari Cribbs, Tracy Larsen, and Ryan Scheife.

Introduction

It is time to power up our thinking. With power thinking comes an increase in our personal growth. *Think Like an Attorney* provides a proven method of thought for the average thinker who no longer wishes to be average. Average equates to the "C" student and they seem to be winning.

I believe there is a need for stronger thinking, given the relaxed and hyper-casual atmosphere in society today. Formal thinking seems to have fallen by the wayside in favor of easy thinking. Centuries of time honored legal principles have been adopted by law schools, attorneys, judges, and juries as a method of problem-solving and decision making. Analytical, dispassionate vehicles of thought have always prevailed in the American legal system. So why not bring these very skills to the nonlawyer? Can't everyone acquire that same edge? The "edge" I speak of refers to mental discipline, unfettered by passion. After 30 years of practicing law, I have observed the benefit of such thought skills. My goal is to assist the nonlawyer in achieving a higher level of thought, compelling one to think in a formal, correct, and above all, dispassionate way.

The law school and subsequent lawyer experience requires truly rigorous exercise of the mind. This lawyerly way of thinking can apply to countless business and personal life scenarios. This book aims to help you make your case in the courtroom of life. We do so by employing reasoned analysis and persuasion. It is critical to understand both sides of an issue before we seek to persuade others to our point of view. Real diversity is understanding the point of view of your opponent. This has the added benefit of improved understanding of our own position. This method of thought inevitably leads to increased achievement and the ultimate result: increased self-value in the market place. Lawyerly thinking is reasonable and confident thinking and it shows.

I come from four generations of attorneys. I graduated from law school in 1985 and have practiced law for over thirty years in the family business. We exclusively represented personal injury clients. I was very proud to advocate for the "little guy" against powerful insurance companies. This David v. Goliath philosophy was and is very important to me. But most important, I was honored to help my clients during a very troubled period in their lives. I literally saw my clients change from troubled and fearful to confident and assured. The legal journey that we took together was truly transformative for them. I essentially trained my clients in the basics of injury law. I prepared them for depositions against aggressive defense lawyers. I shepherded them through the settlement/mediation process. Ultimately, I prepared my clients for their own trial. That trial was their one shot at compensation for an injustice suffered.

At the end of the legal process my clients walked out of my office taller than when they walked in. They did so because they had learned some truly valuable legal thought skills that they could use long after their case ended. By the end, my clients understood the hows and whys of their own case. I say to you now that I am truly proud of all of my clients. I not only represented them, but I coached them through many difficulties, directly and indirectly related to their lawsuit. I helped them navigate complexities of the legal system. In every sense of the term, I acted as a life coach for their legal and nonlegal problems. Frankly, it has been my privilege to serve them in both arenas.

During this thirty-year legal journey, I have realized that law and legal thought are not only transformative, but transferable. Unlike other professions, such as engineering, medicine, or accounting, law is readily adaptable to business and life. I have learned two things in my career: first, we all need to know a little law; second, anyone can think like a lawyer. Legal rules and dispassionate thinking skills are perfect for solving life's problems, great and small. Knowledge of the law is also a great confidence builder in the bargain.

So, if anyone can think like a lawyer, why not my reader as well? We are all surrounded by laws. Law can be as complex as a Supreme Court decision or as simple as the owner's manual to your lawnmower. Both represent the controlling rules of your situation. Law and legal thinking are powers that we can all harness for our own ends. In addition, law provides an excellent vehicle for personal defense. I write this book with the goal of condensing my knowledge and law practice experiences for my reader.

I seek to provide the most valuable lessons I know of the law for your personal growth and career success. The goal is simply this: the full development of self-reliance and advocacy skills to help yourself first and then others. The best metaphor I can think of is the safety speech that flight attendants give at the beginning of every flight. They carefully instruct that in the event of a sudden loss of cabin pressure, place the oxygen mask over our own face first. Only then do we place the mask over our children. Similarly, I will teach legal thinking skills to empower you first, so that you can then help others second. I truly believe that one can operate confidently in any situation with just a few simple yet powerful thinking skills.

This philosophy is a law-based platform for enhanced thinking. It is adaptable to nonlawyers, paralegals, sales people, corporate executives, business owners, and essentially anyone dealing with life or business problems. In essence, we take the best of law and lawyers and distill it into a set of skills that anyone can use. The premise is simply this: anyone can think like an attorney!

There are three groups of non-attorneys who have successfully learned how to think like attorneys. The first group is law students. They engage in the formal study of law, at the great expense of time and money. They therefore have a substantial personal stake in obtaining their law degree. The law student studies from three to four years and must pass multiple written examinations as well as the bar exam.

The second group consists of clients. Clients learn to think like their attorney as a result of the litigation process. Through continuous exposure to their own attorney, opposing counsel, and the judge, they absorb valuable legal thought skills. Clients, too, have a vested interest in the outcome of their case. That outcome is typically financial.

The third and final group is jurors. The juror is compelled into civic service to decide civil and criminal outcomes at trial. They too are exposed to attorneys and judges over several days or weeks. After the conclusion of testimony and evidence, they are issued written instructions from the judge on how to legally resolve the dispute before them. While the juror does not have a financial interest in the outcome, there is a responsibility to deliver justice.

Once each of these nonattorneys has completed the process, a greater mental acuity takes hold. This results in a whole new empowerment. My primary objective is to provide you with a toolbox of legal thinking skills that you can actually apply to real life. Through proper application of these principles, success is within reach. I define such success as: "walking taller after the correct completion of a difficult task." This is exactly what the three nonattorney groups have achieved. Furthermore, when we walk taller, we are instantly more valuable in the marketplace. I have seen this happen not only with my own clients, but with jurors as well. The genius of lawyerly thinking skills is that they are transferable for immediate use in the courtroom of life.

If you endeavor to employ just some of these legal thought skills, you can become the most reasonable person in the room. The aim is to teach core methods of thought employed by lawyers over the centuries. It is truly a better way of thinking. Attorneys in pop culture, television, and movies give only part of the story, and unfortunately, that part is dramatic and unrealistic. This book will take you to the drama-free zone and prepare you with secrets, tactics, and strategies that lawyers don't want you to know about. Attorneys may have the advantage of a law license, but everyone can improve brain power by learning the thought skills attorneys possess.

Many of us are a bit skeptical when it comes to lawyers. Thoughts of scheming, unjust technicalities, and harsh judges immediately come to mind. With that elephant in the courtroom out of the way, I assure you that this book is designed to teach you only the best of lawyerly thinking. Not all lawyers are bad. In fact, they do a lot of good in the world.

Let me be clear: I love to blab about lawyer secrets! It is these secrets that form the platform for personal growth through legal brain power. I am not asking you to think like an attorney 24/7. This book hits on only the legal basics. An added bonus of mastering such skills is that you won't be pushed around again. Since we all need to know a little law, that's exactly what I will deliver. I recommend that you punctuate your career with these thinking techniques.

As you read this book, I encourage you to go the end of each chapter before you begin it. Here you will find a section entitled Black Letter Law. During law school, my professors would regularly write out "Black Letter Law" on the chalkboard. This refers to undisputed legal rules. Black Letter Law consists of firm legal principles that you can count on. I employ this principle by listing simple takeaways and memorable quotes. Think of each list as the least you need to know. I ask you to read these principles first, to better understand the context of each chapter.

There is one final point for you to consider as you read this book. You will notice that I do not provide many illustrative examples. This is by design. I endeavor to make these guiding thought principles so simple that examples are not necessary. This method, too, is a bit of a hangover from my law school days. Professors would drown us in hypothetical examples *ad nauseam*. Without the mental crutch of examples, you can learn better with application to your own problems. I will endeavor to clarify the law in order to readily apply these techniques to life challenges. I do, however, provide a few "war stories" to keep things interesting.

My objective is to teach you the most fundamental elements of legal thinking. This way of thought will enhance your interaction with others personally and professionally. Frankly, legal thinking is good business. My objective is to take you on a journey with the law student as she evolves into a rookie attorney, then trial attorney, and finally to an ethical veteran lawyer.

Make no mistake—this is process is an evolution of thinking. Each chapter builds on the chapter before it. I will illustrate how nonlawyers such as law students, clients, and jurors can learn how to think like attorneys. If they can think like attorneys, you can, too. Think of me as your "thinking advocate" along this journey. The end result should be self-advocacy, self-reliance, self-defense, and ultimately, self-confidence. As you read, please keep in mind this one guiding principle: we all need to know a little law. As we take these educational steps together, absorb, enjoy, and walk tall.

—Brendan J. Cody, 2018.

CHAPTER 1

Law Student Thinking

You come in here with a skull full of mush and you leave thinking like a lawyer.

—Professor Kingsfield,
(The Paper Chase, 20th Century Fox 1973).

The law school experience is the beginning of all things for aspiring lawyers. We include the law school experience in this chapter to assist you in understanding the origins of legal thought. The notion here is to describe the law school ordeal and in particular, the first year of law school. Admission to law school is no small feat. A strong GPA in college coursework is required. In addition, an equally strong score on the Law School Admission Test (LSAT) is required to enter the gates of law school.

Once admitted, the student will be required to attend classes commencing in August and ending in May. A typical part-time schedule would consist of twelve hours of classroom instruction weekly. Most part-time law students work at a law firm performing clerking duties during the day with classroom instruction at night. Full-time students endure up to sixteen class hours per week. In between classes, the student is immersed in reading and summarizing assigned case decisions. Four hundred pages a week of assigned reading is not unusual.

The first thing required of any first-year student is to learn and absorb an entirely new language. This legalese appears in statutes, rules, and case decisions. Statutes are laws created by Congress or state legislatures. Rules for efficient procedure are created by the courts. Finally, case decisions are written interpretations of said laws and rules by a panel of judges.

This new language requires the student to take the first steps towards becoming a wordsmith. Legal jargon is technical and difficult to read. A legal dictionary must be referenced continually in order to wade through the written decisions. The law school experience requires the student to be fully prepared for each class by reading the assigned lengthy cases for each session. The case decision is the distilled product of an appeal of a trial court decision. The appellate court does not retry the case, but rather applies the law to the facts adduced at trial. The decision contains the relevant facts of the case, the legal arguments of the litigants, the rules of law, and finally, the court's opinion as to the law as applied to facts. This final legal decision results in a well-reasoned work of art. The beauty of the decision is twofold. First, it affords the two parties finality after lengthy litigation. Second, it instructs everyone on how to safely proceed under the law.

This method is invaluable to business affairs because we all must know and apply certain rules and policies. Corporate policies contained in any company handbook are a prime example. It is the law of your company. A failure to follow written company policies can create friction, embarrassment, suspension, or even termination. The worst phrase one can utter is this: "I didn't know." Legal thinking requires us to bone up on the rules of our own game. The game cannot be played effectively without that knowledge.

Lawyers and business professionals alike must "know." As they say, "Ignorance of the law is no excuse." Furthermore, laws and rules must be interpreted with plain and ordinary meaning in mind. Tortured reasoning must be avoided. Common sense interpretation of the written word must prevail. Finally, laws never intend an absurd result. In other words, we must strive to achieve reasonable and lawful results as we read a rule, case decision, or even the company handbook. The goal is to avoid becoming lost in our own arguments at the expense of the reasonable intent of the law.

Classroom instruction begins with the Socratic Method, a question/answer dialogue between professor and student. This method was created by the ancient Greek philosopher, Socrates. It was his belief that we arrive at the truth through questions. This question/answer format essentially corners the student by continuously varying the case facts with hypothetical facts. This is all done in the presence of over one hundred fellow students looking on. They too are anxiously awaiting their turn to be called upon. No one knows who is next on rotation. This demands that every student has read the assigned material. Typically, these assignments number one hundred pages per course.

Law school essentially builds quick-thinking skills via the Socratic Method. The verbal exchange between professor and student demands that the student think on her feet. It is a fast-moving process. It can be an unjust way of learning from the student's perspective. Furthermore, the process can be a real confidence crusher. But the reverse is also true. It can be a great confidence builder over time.

In essence, the student is at the sole mercy of the professor's mind-numbing questions. Socrates, the great philosopher, extolled the virtues of arriving at the truth through questions. Good questions clarify, crystallize, and capture the essence of any legal problem and ultimately the solution. These questions typically start with "What are the facts of the case? What happened in the trial court? Why was the original case decision affirmed or reversed? Suppose we alter the case by adding the following hypothetical facts?"

The law school professor continuously probes and prods the student with question after question, changing the facts ever so slightly to set a new trap for the student. The teacher essentially peppers the student with interminable variances of hypotheticals (mythical story problems), which ultimately corners the student. The ordeal is very much like a final exam only the student's mental skills are on full display in front of their classmates.

The downside of the Socratic Method, unfortunately, is that it leaves the student with no clear resolution of the case. Furthermore, it is recommended that one not take notes on the answers given by a fellow student. The odds are that a student's Socratic answer will never be the basis for an exam question. In addition, there usually is no right answer at the end of such an exchange. One unintended consequence is that the student fails to listen to what is being said in class because he is reading the next case in anticipation of being called on. This teaching method tends to mildly terrorize each student yet compels them to be prepared and to think on their feet. Finally, this method teaches the value of arguing all sides of a legal question. A better pedagogical approach would utilize 50 percent Socratic Method and 50 percent Black Letter Law in order to avoid confusion and promote better retention.

The primary result of law school and its philosophy is to reshape the mind and to reinvent the way we think. Legal education tears down students and then rebuilds them. This is essentially Socratic chemotherapy. The objective is to learn to divorce themselves from their feelings on an issue and trade it for cold, brutal analysis of the problem at hand. Essentially, law students are taught to leave many of their emotions and personal convictions at the classroom door. The law student must reinvent himself, leaving the excitable, emotional self behind. The result is clear and diverse thinking. The old adage about law school is true: the first year they scare you to death; the second year they work you to death; the third year they bore you to death.

The thrust of this chapter is to compress the law school experience into manageable knowledge and advice that anyone can use. This method can be used to solve life's problems. The professor continuously varies the "what if" type of hypothetical for the class. The goal is to paint the hapless students into a "Socratic corner" with no escape. The imaginary facts and scenarios force the student to apply the law to multiple situations. The process sharpens the student's "mental game", as it were.

While hypotheticals are quite valuable in the safety of a classroom, they are not so in the real world. The critical nature of the hypothetical is that it has not happened yet, and is in fact, unlikely to ever happen. In the real world, we must deal with only one set of facts that are frighteningly real. The point here is to avoid being dragged into a never-ending litany of hypothetical questions. Such hypos are simply a power play at your expense. Your questioner will never be satisfied with your answer anyway. The best advice is to refuse to engage in hypothetical questions, period. The real world is difficult enough.

The typical case book method requires students to analyze court decisions. The cases provide a number of real life fact patterns between two parties who are contesting their case in a court of law. The forum can be criminal court where freedom is at stake, or civil court, where money damages are at stake. There are always disputes, and there are always legal issues. In the business field, these disputes almost always concern a financial interest where damages are the remedy. In an effort to understand these cases, law students employ the use of timelines, which place a chronology of events in their proper order. Furthermore, students will utilize flow charts to identify the parties and their role in the fact situation. It is essentially connecting the dots in order to better demonstrate, via a flow chart, the facts of the case. In law school, as in actual law practice, this ability to "timeline" and "flow chart" the facts is critical to understanding what is happening in a complex fact pattern. This will be discussed in greater detail in Chapter 4.

Cumulative final examinations are the rule in law school. For instance, a criminal law course will typically begin in August with a Christmas break in December and end the following May. Then, a four-hour final examination is held to test the students' cumulative knowledge over that nine month period. Students' test grade will rise and fall on the results of the one examination.

Unfortunately for law students, with no tests during the academic year, they will have little feedback by which to gauge their progress. This "all or nothing" method is truly a metaphor for life's failure to give us the feedback we desire. This demands that we overcompensate in the learning department to ensure that nothing is missed. This cumulative method requires one to accomplish the following:

- **A.** To manage a vast amount of information;
- **B.** To condense that information into critical bullet points and black letter law;
- **C.** To apply the law to fictional story problems; and
- **D.** To keep current on assigned reading.

In order to facilitate these four goals, students will employ a study outline. This is a skeletal outline of the most important concepts from each class. This mnemonic device triggers the most important rules that must be applied to examination questions. Basic rules of law require memorization, as do the exceptions to those general rules. The study outline consists of very brief case summaries and black letter law incorporated with classroom notes. All of this material must be thoroughly digested for a successful attack on the final examination. A typical outline of a sample contract law topic illustrates the point:

Contract Law

Case Title: *Smith v. Jones*

Short Factual Statement: The parties enter into a written non-disclosure agreement for $130,000.

Rules of Law: offer, acceptance, consideration, meeting of the minds, enforceable contract.

Exceptions to Rules of Law: fraud; failure to execute document, unenforceable contract.

Application: rule is applied to hypothetical fact pattern.

I recall my first law school examination at my alma mater, William Mitchell College of Law in St. Paul, Minnesota. As professor Steenson handed out the exams, he also handed us some sage advice. The first was this: If you have a "reasonable belief" that you are about to vomit, terminate the exam! He was very clear that the reasonable prudent person standard even applies to barfing! Very inspiring.

The second, more practical advisory was this: dispose of the issue. He explained that you cannot stay fixated on one question when other exam questions are waiting. This is particularly important in a timed exam. He emphasized the critical nature of moving on instead of dwelling on one question. I have returned to this advice over and over again. It has enabled me to leave behind dead issues in favor of moving on to new challenges and new projects. Such a philosophy prevents us from staying in the same place forever. It truly demands a focus on the present, and not dwelling the past.

Now comes the infamous law school examination itself. The best way to capture the intensity and preparation for the exam comes from a quote from Scott Turow's book, *One-L* (Farrar, Straus and Giroux 1977). Mr. Turow was a Harvard law student in 1976. Some of his tools may seem outdated by today's standards, but I think you will get the general idea.

> Then I went into the test room. I came to these four-hour numbers with a virtual traveling commissary: Earplugs, paper, four pencils, four pens, three rolls of mints, two packs of cigarettes, a cup of iced coffee, a Coke, 2 chocolate bars, a pencil sharpener, an extension cord for my typewriter. (p. 267.)

A typical four-hour examination consists of a number of story problems. These story problems contain fact situations that contain a number of legal issues. Not unlike an Easter egg hunt, the student must seek out and identify the relevant legal issues. After the facts are presented, a common question will be asked: "What are the rights and obligations of the parties?" Finally, the most important question: "Who wins and why?"

First of all, the rights and obligations of the parties refers to that portion of the law that bestows an entitlement with the force of law to protect it. For instance, we all have the constitutional right to be free of an unreasonable search and seizure by the state. Warrantless searches of our homes are prohibited, and for good reason. Further, each party has obligations or legal duties, regardless of who brings the claim. An illustration of a legal duty revolves around the simple task of driving a motor vehicle. As drivers, we all have a legal duty of care in the proper operation, lookout, speed, and control of our vehicle on public roadways. These rights and corresponding obligations of both parties are the foundation of any analysis of the case facts.

The second question, who wins and why, recognizes that there are clear winners and losers in life. While litigants have their strengths and weaknesses, the judge and jury can award to only one party. During the test, law students must pick a side and explain why their side wins. The "who wins and why" scenario compels the examinee to offer the best legal advice for a hypothetical client. In real life, courts cannot engage in endless debate about who is right or wrong. There must be finality for every case. The courts award an objective measure of damages in the form of dollars. With such an objective amount, there is no doubt as to who has won and who has lost.

A reliable formula for answering these exam questions is identified by the acronym IRAC:

I = Issue
R = Rule
A = Analysis
C = Conclusion

This template requires students to present their answers in a standardized form. This feature forces the student to think in an orderly, standardized fashion. Think of it as a form or checklist. Templates will be used not only through law school, but throughout the lawyer's entire career. Templates will be covered in depth in Chapter 2. Suffice it to say, the template assists the student in providing their professor with a standardized outline for their answer. It enables the law school professor to examine and evaluate the law student's answer at a glance. The evaluation of the student will rise and fall on whether or not the student identifies the proper issues and thereafter applies the proper rule of law to the facts.

A typical fact situation will involve a client with a legal problem presented to his lawyer. The facts will come from an initial interview type of situation. Once the issue or true controversy is identified, the proper rule of law must be applied to the facts. Both sides of the controversy must be addressed. These involve claims and defenses. The conclusion requires the student to take a winning side and argue it persuasively. The examinee takes a stand on the question after analyzing both sides of the controversy. The student analyzes all sides before reaching a well thought out conclusion.

This is a true crystallization process with an equally pure result. Identification first, analysis second, and persuasion last. Any problem on earth can be solved by the proper application of this method. In the truest sense, this is a problem-solving formula in a nutshell. Lastly, IRAC serves the dual purpose of an outline for the teacher and student. As students formulate an answer, they can provide a skeletal version of the IRAC template listing the highlights of the written answer to come. This is typically included on the inside cover of the test booklet and serves as a table of contents for the professor. Thus, the teacher knows if students are on the right track from the beginning.

The following vignette is an example of the application of IRAC in the real world. Your daughter has just been suspended by her principal for a violation of the school disciplinary code. The school does allow you to present your child's side of the story before the suspension actually takes effect. The first step is to identify the main issue. Does your daughter's behavior actually violate the disciplinary code? This is the primary issue. The next step is to obtain a copy of the disciplinary code itself. The point is to identify the applicable rule that she is alleged to have violated. The third step is to apply the rule to her behavior. Her story and the statements of witnesses must all be factored in. The application of the rule to the facts translates into an analysis of the case. An important note here is that the school's side and the student's side must be given equal focus. This is analytical diversity. This is seeing the case from the other guy's perspective.

Finally, one must take a stand on the analysis and come to a conclusion. This means choosing the argument that you feel is most persuasive based on the evidence. You have now taken a side. The lesson for all of us is that we must regularly grapple with life's little story problems. So we use an orderly method to solve them. Finally, if one can argue a given side of a coin, one must develop the ability to argue the reverse side of that coin. This is not only a well-rounded approach, but mentally diverse. The ability to be fluent concerning both sides of an argument promotes a deeper understanding of the entire matter.

There is a final point regarding IRAC that should be considered. There is a variation of this formula known as CREAC:

C=Conclusion
R=Rule
E=Explanation
A=Application
C=Conclusion

This variant of the original formula seeks to provide the professor with the conclusion first. This avoids unnecessary suspense as to where the student is going with his answer. By putting the conclusion out front, the message is that much easier to follow. Knowledge of the conclusion first, shapes the entire context of the narrative that follows. If you really want to make a friend out of your reader or audience, get to the point immediately by setting forth your conclusion first and then explain it. By the way, courts regularly employ the CREAC formula for clarity and consistency in their decisions.

Legal research and writing is a separate course, entirely different from the traditional core courses. This class simulates the representation of a client's interests on appeal. The course requires a student to research real court cases and then apply them to various hypothetical fact situations. After the students conduct their research they then write a brief. Once again, they must utilize another template:

- Facts
- Procedural posture (The path that the case has traveled at each phase of the legal system)
- Issues
- Argument (Citation to the law/legal authority)
- Conclusion

If this sounds familiar, it should. It is almost the identical template of the IRAC checklist. Once again, we have a useful and orderly method of problem solving. The appellate brief we are discussing must be submitted to a panel of several judges. Their function is not to retry the case, but review possible errors by the trial court judge. The lesson here is that law students are taught that outlines and templates are critical to organized legal thinking and presentation. Once the brief is complete, the student will be ready to engage in an oral presentation of the case. They must know their facts and present arguments accordingly. This process is known as oral argument.

Oral argument typically allows students to present their case in a timed format, usually fifteen minutes. Their opponent is allowed the same amount of time to respond. Much like Socratic chemotherapy, the student will be peppered with questions from a three-judge panel. Again, the objective is to seek the truth through questioning. They will make the presentation in a mock courtroom. The experience is designed to simulate the battle conditions of a real appellate courtroom, with all of its formalities, procedural rules, and courtroom decorum.

There is no greater adversity than that presented in a court of appeals argument. The judges will repeatedly interrupt the presentation of the law student. They will do so without apology. Instead of a single professor, the student now faces three judges who will bombard him with questions, hypotheticals, and general criticism. The judges may even pull a "reverse" and require the student to argue their opponent's case and vice versa. After all this occurs, the students may attack each other's position.

Personal attacks on each other is expressly discouraged. This is essentially a trial by fire requiring both students to think on their feet and to parry various thrusts and attacks on their client's case. With each oral argument and with each classroom Socratic experience, the student gains a deeper understanding of ordered legal thought while under pressure. The true value to such difficult experiences is the confidence and competence that a student gains by thinking under fire. By being forced to give quick, unemotional responses, the student learns to give a reasoned argument despite external pressures.

Additional courses, such as trial advocacy (simulated jury trials), as well as advanced courses, become typical fare in the remaining two-to-three years of law school once the first year is completed. Elective courses such as Taxation, Corporations, Worker's Compensation, and Family Law are some examples. Once the students have survived the rigors of law school, they will graduate with a Juris Doctorate. Strong grades are required to gain employment with top law firms. On the entrepreneurial end of the spectrum, some even create their own law firms. However, none of this occurs until the student successfully complete the bar examination.

After graduation, the freshly minted juris doctor must engage in a sixty-day learning process known as the bar review. The course I took was named BAR/BRI. This course was created by a lawyer by the name of Richard Conviser. His purpose was to provide an organized format of review for the state bar examination. This course was in a word: superior. It is the finest crash course out there.

The BAR/BRI course lasts sixty days, Monday through Friday with two to three hours of lecture each day. Students are given written materials consisting of near-perfect outlines of core law school classes and sample bar exam questions. This "crash course" is designed to present a power review of major classes covered in law school over the past three to four years.

After the first week of this intense review, I wanted to kick some of my old professors right in the pants. Gone was the Socratic Method, and in its place was clear, spoon-fed law. There were no more intimidating questions. No more vague explanations. Just Black Letter Law. Unvarnished legal knowledge is the order of the day in such a course. Vince Lombardi once said: "Discard the immaterial." He may have been referring to law as well as football. With an exam of such magnitude occurring in only 60 days, time is of the essence. This supports the rule that only the relevant and material survives.

The review course demands rote memory. Critical legal formulas and concepts must be memorized. The notion here is that certain rules are, by their very nature, clear and undisputed. Therefore one can proceed safely as long as the rule is followed. This is an important career lesson that advances the notion that certain formulas, rules, and theories must be committed to memory. This old school rote memorization keeps the knowledge readily at hand. Furthermore, timed sample tests are given periodically in order to simulate the "battlefield conditions" of an actual bar exam. Repeated application of laws to story problems is the rule. Since this exam is timed, it requires speedy thinking under pressure. These practice exams are invaluable to the student, for they provide a certain strengthening of the mind for sustained hours of exam writing. It is not just what you know that counts, but how well you can apply the rules of law as well.

I cannot recommend enough this brand of compressed learning. Compressed courses or crash courses make us learn more efficiently and intensely. If there is any crash course that you can get hold of, sign up for it. Life is short. Crash course it! That is what this book is all about. It is intended as a crash course in legal thinking for career success.

Once you complete any such course, you go out into the world confidently armed with the basic knowledge to pass any test that they can throw at you. Always be on the lookout for a great accelerated course on a valuable topic. This can cover either a personal interest or more importantly, a professional one. The point here is that such courses or seminars are a fast track to personal growth and development.

Now comes the bar exam itself. Each state requires a passing score on the bar exam in order to practice law. This ensures minimum standards of competency in order to protect the public. A typical bar examination is a two-day challenge requiring the test taker to answer essay questions as well as multiple choice questions. Typically the essay questions will again consist of fact situations and issues directed at one particular law school discipline. Examples are criminal procedure, contracts, torts, and civil procedure.

Ordinarily, the exam consists of four questions for the morning session and four questions for the afternoon session. Each exam question is loaded with issues and potential traps. The goal is to identify the legal issues and then apply the correct law to resolve the conflict. Once again, one must answer the eternal question: "Who wins and why?"

On day two of the examination, the multiple-choice section requires the student to examine short questions with four to five possible choices. The trick is to select "the best answer." Many of the answers are correct, but the most correct answer is the only one that counts. It consists of one hundred questions in the morning and one hundred questions in the afternoon. Three hours are allowed for each session. The examinee is then notified of the results within two to three months. Once all of these rigors are completed, the law student is now ready to transition to her role as a rookie lawyer. She can now commence the practice of law as well as student loan payments.

A final positive observation deserves merit. The law school experience builds not only legal minds but great relationships as well. Law students form a deep bond with each other. They have been through a three-year war and have lived to tell about it. Friendships forged through such a difficult experience last for decades. Collegial relationships form as well. Many business referrals originate from connections made in law school. Lawyers often call their former professors years later for consultation and advice. These ongoing connections are arguably some of the most valuable products of a law school education.

BLACK LETTER LAW

- Court decisions provide finality and predictability so that one can proceed correctly and safely.
- The Socratic Method seeks to arrive at truth through questions.
- Classroom hypotheticals clarify and at the same time trap the unwitting law student.
- Law school exam questions ask: Who wins and why? There are clear winners and losers in court and in life.
- We all must read, know, and apply our company handbook. Be sure to know it backwards and forwards.
- Civil courts determine money damages as a remedy. Criminal courts determine freedom or imprisonment.
- IRAC and CREAC are two great formulas that provide an orderly format for problem solving.
- Always be on the make for a great crash course for accelerated learning. Life's short. Crash course it.
- Meaningful preparation demands that you are able to try the other guy's case, too.
- Do not stay fixated on one problem or event forever. Move on to the next issue with all deliberate speed.
- The law student outline is a tool for managing vast amounts of information.
- In life many answers are correct, but you must select the *most* correct answer.

CHAPTER 2

Rookie Attorney Thinking

Once the ex-law student becomes a licensed attorney, he will be vested with all of the obligations and privileges of an attorney at law. He can now actually represent clients in the marketplace and the courtroom. Once lawyers are admitted to the bar, they are held to the same professional standards as a forty-year veteran. We will define the term "Rookie Attorney" as an attorney with five years of experience or less. These years are literally marked by trial and error. This chapter illustrates that all things have a beginning and that we learn by doing. We must graduate sometime. The student must move from the safety of the library to the high-risk environment of the courtroom. Mistakes will be made, but without such mistakes there is limited growth. The goal of this chapter is to help us learn from the struggles of the novice attorney for our own advantage.

The rookie attorney knows just enough to be dangerous. With no experience and no track record, they must stumble through real cases presented by real clients. The good news is that this is the second step in an evolution of professional thought skills. Once again, they must identify the legal issues presented by a client's complex fact pattern. Mind you, the civilian client has no idea what the proper issues are. These must be identified by the new lawyer, and hopefully he has a strong mentor to assist in identifying these issues.

Typically a first-year associate is assigned a partner who acts as a mentor. This mentor will assign various tasks, research projects, court appearances, depositions, and client meetings to their young charge. The struggle here is to learn by doing. As Confucius said: "I hear and I forget. I see and I remember. I do and I understand." With each completed assignment, the rookie lawyer gains more and more experience and confidence in his own ability. The actual art of doing is critical. The attorney mentor can be crucial to the early successes of the rookie attorney. A great mentor contributes a judicious mixture of criticism and praise. A proper pairing with a solid mentor can compress years of experience into a short period of time. Unfortunately, there will be plenty of defeats in the early going.

The law school experience was essentially focused on simulated court appearances, as well as legal theories. These experiences all occurred within the safety of a classroom. Now the new lawyer must deal with real world problems in real time. The outcome is legal victory or defeat for the client. This is a very serious undertaking when a client's one chance rides on their attorney's skill and ability. Furthermore, if it is a criminal matter, the undertaking is even greater as the client's freedom is at stake.

As the new lawyer begins their career, they will find that they must master a whole new area of expertise. In order to gain expertise, one must engage in extensive research into their chosen field of practice. This research takes many forms. A ready source comes from files already worked on by other attorneys in the law firm. Instead of running to a lawyer for guidance, ideally one should look to the written work already compiled in a client master file. Such files are full of correspondence, court filings, court rulings, document requests, and deposition transcripts. Such resources provide invaluable "how to" examples by those who have been there and done it. The rookie attorney can imitate such examples and incorporate them into his own practice.

The first instinct for most of us is to look for help from someone else. Not so with attorneys. They are taught early on to figure out the problem on their own. Self-research is the bedrock of self-reliance. Self-reliance requires that one struggle with and research the issue alone, without assistance. This has the added effect of instilling self-confidence. Self-reliance is an authentic skill, which navigates us successfully through life. It is much more meaningful to work it through on one's own than to be handed the answer on a silver platter. It is the painful learning process that promotes growth.

We can all learn from the legal experience. The goal is to resist the temptation to look to others for help right away. The objective should be to conduct your own private research on your problem or issue. Once you do this, you will command greater respect from that person you may seek out for that final answer. Remember: repeated requests for help diminish you in the eyes of others. The final benefit of self-research is that the process will ingrain experience and expertise that would otherwise be lost.

This new environment requires the young lawyer to think and learn on the run. Inevitably, mistakes will be made, but this is essential to the learning process. The hope is that these mistakes will be *de minims* or so minor as not to damage the client's case. The goal of the young lawyer is to avoid making mistakes that cost his client or cause in court. For instance, in the field of medicine, the first and foremost objective of every doctor is to "first, do no harm." This quote is applicable to rookie attorneys, as well as physicians. The paradox here is this: learning from mistakes is essential for experience. One must force these two concepts to live together and achieve a delicate balance between them.

With each case, with each court appearance, the young lawyer reaches a greater level of confidence and competence in his abilities. The trick for any new lawyer is to make it a rule to never get behind on their caseload or assignments. The young lawyer and his early career are both marked by reactivity. By this we mean that the lawyer at this stage is in a constant state of being reactive to problems and grass fires that need to be extinguished. Instead of taking a proactive stance, which the veteran lawyer employs, the young lawyer simply reacts and attempts to solve each problem as it comes along. The new lawyer must not wait for that bad thing to come, but rather intercept it first. This notion keeps the attorney ahead of her files. Unfailing preparation is key. In business, as well as law, control your files so they don't control you.

The major problem with the rookie lawyer is that in many instances he does not have a strong mentor and, when left to his own devices the result can be incompetence at some level. The mere license to practice law does not make a competent lawyer. This license simply means that the new lawyer has met the minimum standards of competency. This particular problem is most acute with the solo practitioner rookie lawyer. The object lesson here is that one must seek out and find one who has been there and done that before. A reliable mentor provides the rookie with a wealth of wisdom in half the time.

A further concern for the young lawyer is the mastering of an entirely new specialty of law. This law could be personal injury, workers compensation, bankruptcy, marital dissolution, corporate law, or criminal law, among others. The young lawyer will have to learn not only the law on the subject, but practical applications, as well. This type of knowledge can be acquired through continuing legal education seminars that require a lawyer to update their skill set. These seminars provide written materials authored by lawyers for lawyers. The seminars are typically directed at a specific practice area. The day of the general practitioner is long gone. Regular updates in the changing landscape of one's area of expertise are essential. New developments can be found in trade journals, online updates, classes, annual conventions, and seminars, for example. Such self-updating must be as regular as those in our cell phones and computers. These updates fix the "bugs" in our self development. Whenever the opportunity arises, learn from someone who has already been there.

Seven Deadly Sins of the Rookie Attorney That We All Can Learn From

There are seven deadly sins committed at one time or another by the novice lawyer, so here they are:

1. The unreturned phone call, text, or e-mail. This creates unnecessary friction, bad blood, and the feeling of being ignored. The solution is this: return all communications within 24 hours.

2. Failure to follow up. You have made such a great first impression. Then, for some reason, you fail to follow up on your great momentum. If you do not follow up, that potentially great customer, contact, or opportunity, will be lost forever. Simple follow-up e-mails, texts, letters or phone calls do the job. Stay in front of your customer intermittently so you are not forgotten.

3. Lateness. Follow Vince Lombardi Time: arrive at least 15 minutes ahead of every scheduled event. Any later and you are late.

4. Failure to prepare. Remember Prof. Kingsfield from The Paper Chase? Responsibility for the written materials in class is nonnegotiable.

5. Disorder. "Heaven's 1st law is order."-Pope. Hell's 1st law is chaos. Keep your desk and files in order at all times.

6. Procrastination. Is it really "leadership for tomorrow?" Not a chance. All things must be done with immediacy. This includes your own assignments. It also includes the speedy delivery of bad news to the boss. All bosses insist on hearing bad news immediately. If the problem

is caught in time, it can be remedied. The remedy delayed is the remedy denied.

7. Unfamiliarity with law or procedure. This refers to rules of legal substance and rules of courtroom practice. One cannot play the game if one does not know the rules. Be sure to know the rules of your company and industry. Self-education is key. We all have a duty to read and to know.

The Partner Memo

A good persuasive memo to the boss is critical to the survival of a young associate climbing the way up the ladder. A memo is a written document that memorializes research directed at a given problem. Generally, it is a factual problem that requires solution. Typically, the associate must do legal research regarding the problem at hand.

This involves researching case law, which are appellate decisions made by a panel of judges. It can also involve rules of civil procedure, as well as statutes. The partner memo also serves to document events, actions, and mental impressions of the case. If an attorney leaves, retires, or even dies, all efforts will live on for the next attorney to simply read and apply. The wheels of the case will not have to be reinvented. This is invaluable for the effective representation of the client.

A typical memo template consists of the following:

I. Facts
II. Issues
III. Analysis/Application of law to facts
IV. Opinion
V. Conclusions with recommended course of action

This sounds familiar because it is very similar to the template used for law school examinations known as IRAC. Old habits die hard, but a complete memorandum will live forever. The memo, as we can see, is a tightly ordered memorandum of law that will enable the partner to address the key legal issues in any problem the client presents. This memo can be used as a foundation for the evaluation of the case itself. Should the author of the memo leave the firm or be transferred to a different case, the succeeding lawyer can pick up the file and read that memo and have a thorough and immediate understanding of the case. The memo essentially encapsulates the pros, cons, weaknesses, strengths, and crucial details of the case. It is a detailed sketch of the most important components of the file.

I am not suggesting that you follow this exact template as far as your own memos are concerned. However, there are elements from this memorandum that can help you in your daily business and personal dealings. Memos are important as they capture the essence of an event and even the emotion of the moment. Memos capture and crystalize important events. They should be typed or dictated immediately after the event, be it a meeting, a phone call, or other significant occurrence. Such memoranda are particularly useful to memorialize a meeting with your doctor, lawyer, realtor, boss, co employees, or even a parent teacher conference. When created immediately, it instills solid credibility in the drafter. A typical memo template for non-lawyers should include the following:

Event title
Names of attendees
Date of memo
Date of event or conversation
Start time
Finish time
Location
To

From
Topic
Purpose and substance of meeting
Summary of contributions by participants
Analysis
Conclusions
Recommended course of action

The substance of the memo details contributions from the participants at the meeting or phone call. This also involves documentation of any authority that a participant has cited for their position that can be reviewed at a later date. Such authorities may consist of the company handbook, articles, books, trade journals, internet research, relevant documents, and the like. These authorities should be cross-checked to confirm their accuracy. Always try to obtain authoritative sources.

The core of the memo should contain past history. For instance, has this issue occurred before, and if so, what was the outcome in a same or similar situation? Refer to that document and incorporate it by reference. In the memorandum, be certain to capture the attitude, demeanor, and tone of the participants. This serves to humanize the event. Beware, however, that if you are making written observations of such attitudes, the participants may see this memo at a later date. One may even consider creating a private supplemental memo on personal observations, so as not to offend.

The purpose section of the memo, as we can see, is to capture the events that have transpired. It should also include the "hows and whys" of the event. These memos may be read months or even years later and therefore must recreate the event in detail. Lawyers typically use memos in order to refresh their own memories as well those of clients and witnesses. This is known as a "past recollection recorded." Typically, memorandums in attorney/client files are work product. This refers to the private and creative thoughts of an attorney, which are hers and hers alone. Work product is legally protected from being disclosed to the other side. The memorandum also documents the lawyer's mental impressions of the case. Although lawyers may enjoy protection regarding their work product, you may not. A lawyer has a great deal of latitude when it comes to capturing and preserving his own thoughts and ideas. Nonlawyers do not have that particular luxury, so exercise due care in your own drafting.

There are three rules that one should follow at any important meeting. First, take care as to what you say. Second, document what you say. Third, document what they say. In addition, the memo, as you can see, must be quite detailed. This brings us to a fourth rule: the greater the detail, the greater the veracity. This simply means that by detailing the description of important events, any critic will be hard pressed to dispute its accuracy. Such fine detail certifies that you are not manufacturing facts.

There is even an exception to the hearsay rule in jury trials known as the "business record" exception. This evidentiary rule allows the introduction of "records kept in the ordinary course of business" for a jury to examine. The notion is that such business records are inherently reliable even though the author is not present to testify. The device of the memo is essentially a template. Lawyers love templates. Judges revere them. The court system is dependent upon them. The template, checklist, or form has proven its effectiveness over time. In sum, the memo prevents missing the crucial and relevant components of an event. It is a uniform template that is standardized and predictable for everyone.

It is important that the memorandum be completed immediately after the event while facts and events are still fresh in one's mind. The memorandum should give a date and time as to when it was generated. A memorandum completed within one week of the event is less effective than one done within minutes of the event. The great Chinese philosopher Confucius says that we cannot rely on memory alone to reconstruct an event. He states: "The palest ink is better than the most retentive memory." This quote illustrates that the passage of time truly erodes the memory of the event. We cannot forget the value of "the palest ink."

Memorandums require immediate creation. Do not procrastinate on a memorandum. Capture the event while it is still fresh in your mind. The bottom line value of any such memo is this: you may need it someday! There is nothing more valuable than this "past recollection recorded." It is a valuable self-protection tool as well. This self-protection tool serves to document that you have done your job thoroughly if you are challenged later.

Deposition Skills

One of my first official appearances as a rookie attorney involved the deposition. Prior to my first deposition, I attended several of them with an attorney mentor. The deposition is a question/answer session designed to obtain information from a plaintiff, defendant, or witness. It can last from two hours to a full day. This device is part of the discovery process in every lawsuit. This device preserves a sworn statement from the deponent. It is a highly structured method of communication between two individuals, the questioning attorney and the witness. The other persons present are the lawyer representing the witness and the court reporter.

The goal is to "discover" as much information as possible from your opponent before trial. This sworn deposition requires deep preparation of the client. After all, the client is under oath so there are no retakes. Some lawyers have their client watch an instructional video as their sole preparation. I do not believe in such "one size fits all" approaches. Deposition prep should involve methodical and complete discussion with the client days before the statement. The client is briefed with important documents and records in order to fully educate him on the facts of his own case. If the deponent misremembers important facts, this will spell trouble for him. In most cases, the inaccurate answer will translate into untruthfulness. Remember that lawyers are always the first to think the worst.

The preparation of each client involves, to a large extent, their own personal history. This would include name, addresses, marital status, educational, and employment background. In the personal injury case, the client's version of the accident itself as well as physical complaints is very important. Timelines of past relevant injuries and lawsuits are covered as well. The personal facts of each client are all unique, but the deposition rules themselves are not. The rules of a deposition are rules of formality that apply to an "under oath conversation" between two individuals. These rules impose order and facilitate a clean typed record for later use by the attorneys and ultimately the judge and jury. Simply put, the deposition is a civil and orderly approach to human conversation. It demands two-way communication at the clearest level possible. These rules are fairly simple and straightforward.

The first rule of the deposition is this: two people cannot talk at the same time. It is impossible for the court reporter to record two people speaking at the same time. Anticipating the question before it is completed is not allowed. This is a great lesson for human conversation. This rule forces you to think about the question, wait, and then answer. It is a methodical process that prevents one from interrupting when they think they have the answer. If you interrupt, then you are not listening. The rule prevents us from mentally getting ahead of the questioner and promotes focus on one question at a time. By waiting for the questioner to actually finish the question, we prevent miscommunication. It is also great manners to refrain from talking over another person.

An additional point here is that humans cannot hold two thoughts in their mind simultaneously. We can hold only one thought at a time in our heads. So many times I see people talking right over someone else in conversation. Neither person is actually listening to the other. Therefore we must speak one at a time so as to avoid confusion. So focus only on the question and then your answer.

The second rule of the deposition asserts that if you answer the question, then you understood it. This requires you to alert your questioner if you do not understand the question. This enables the question to be rephrased or clarified. If you do not speak up for yourself in a timely fashion, you cannot complain later that your own answer is wrong. This rule also promotes clear communication during the conversation. It also holds you responsible for your own answer. The lesson is this: never answer a question that you don't understand. If you are a little fuzzy, ask that the question be rephrased.

A third rule requires us to speak clearly and audibly. Nods or shakes of the head are not allowed as they are ambiguous. Spelling of names and technical terms is also encouraged. Again, it is critical to communicate clearly not cryptically. Fourth, guessing is not allowed. It is valueless to guess on any matter. If you don't know, then say so. No one is expected to be able to have an answer to every question. Reasonable or educated estimates are allowed, however.

A final point on depositions concerns advocacy. Short of an actual trial, there is no greater arena where the lawyer displays advocacy skills. To illustrate the point, I refer to one of my own past clients, Stevie Broberg. Stevie was a worker's compensation client. He had a severe injury to his arm and brought a claim for damages. He also was a brittle diabetic, which exacerbated his work injury. During his deposition Stevie began to suffer from diabetes-related low blood sugar. In the middle of some very stressful and demanding questioning, he grew very confused and began to tremble. His blood sugar was plummeting. We took an immediate recess and adjourned to my private office.

Stevie was in real trouble, but he knew how to handle it. He pulled from his backpack a stash of cookies and began to quickly consume them. This was his emergency supply of sugar. He was prepared.

This was a simple solution to a very complex medical problem. As he began to feel better, he offered me a cookie. I gladly accepted and we nibbled on our cookies waiting for the storm to pass. This was my first true lesson in advocacy. I acted as constant legal companion to my client. I hope that my presence was as comforting to him as that sugar cookie.

The simple art of standing with someone and standing for someone is the essence of advocacy. The client must never walk through litigation alone. Stevie and I went back in and successfully completed that deposition. That was my first deposition. I learned in one day the power of advocacy. It is the greatest gift that you can give to your boss, co-employees, and your customer. It is the simple knowledge that you are their unwavering ally and you will not leave their side. There is one sad footnote however to this story: Stevie died only a few short years later of complications from diabetes. I will never forget him nor our first deposition.

Ten Self-Protection Skills for Rookie Lawyers and You, Too

Crucial skills that a rookie lawyer must develop early on are those of self-protection. Such skills are confidence building and empowering. I conclude this chapter with a short checklist that we all can use:

1. Absorb more information than you give out. Use the age-old proportion of two ears and one mouth. Listen twice as much as you speak. By listening and withholding, you not only control the flow of information, but you become more of a mystery. An open book is a wonderful thing, but don't be one yourself!

2. Avoid making guarantees. There are too many variables that you cannot control in business and life.

3. Try the other guy's case in your head. This is very helpful when it comes to your opponent as well as the judge or other decision maker. This is true diversity. It leads to well-rounded knowledge of all facets of your case. "Prepare as those around you would." You must know your opponent's case. It is not just about what you think, but what the other side thinks, as well. Get into his head and prepare accordingly. Don't be self-centered or self-involved in just your own case. See the big picture.

4. Keep your own work product and mental impressions secret. This is also known as the "theory of your case." The attorney has his protected by law. You do not. So defend yourself by not blabbing your best ideas and business trade secrets.

5. Distinguish between book smarts and street smarts. Not all theories work in real life. A hybrid of the two is best.

6. "Trust but Verify," President Reagan. Be sure to fact-check the most important and controversial information with multiple independent sources. Take no one's word for it. Trust the information given to you initially, but verify it before you draw any final conclusions.

7. Research the problem on your own first. Do so thoroughly. This is active self-reliance. It will also get you the respect of your colleagues. Ask for help as a last resort, not a first resort.

8. Engage in regular continuing education in your field to stay on top of current developments.

9. Be the first to think the worst. This is truly the power of negative thinking. Smart cynicism requires us to anticipate the worst-case scenarios in business. When analyzing a problem, privately assume the worst and work backwards from there. Given the profit motive in today's world, we cannot assume that everyone has the best of intentions.

10. Lawyers cannot represent the world. Ethically and legally, they can represent just the one client. With the limitations of time and space, we simply cannot be all things to all people. Focus on your own corner of the world and advocate for it with vigor.

BLACK LETTER LAW

- The rookie attorney knows just enough to be dangerous. We learn by defeat. We learn by doing. Link up with a strong mentor. Seek out and find someone who has already been there and done that.
- Self-research is the bedrock of self-reliance.
- Avoid the 7 deadly sins of the rookie attorney.
- Legal thinking is an evolutionary process.
- The remedy delayed is the remedy denied.
- A complete memorandum captures and crystalizes any meeting or event.
- The greater the detail the greater the veracity.
- "The palest ink is better than the most retentive memory"- Confucius.
- Deposition rules encourage great listening and speaking. Both must be done one at a time.
- Advocate for others. Never let them walk alone.
- Attorneys cannot represent the world. Neither can you. Endeavor to protect your own little corner of the world.
- An open book is a wonderful thing but don't be one yourself.
- Be the first to think the worst.
- Always seek out a form or a template whenever possible. Chances are the problem has already come up before and someone has already invented a form for it.
- Repeated requests for help diminish you in the eyes of your colleagues.

- Don't forget the ten self-protection skills for business and personal success.
- "I hear and I forget. I see and I remember. I do and I understand".- Confucius.

CHAPTER 3

Trial Attorney Thinking

This chapter addresses the more advanced thinking skills of judges and trial lawyers. It involves an introduction to a number of basic legal concepts. Not unlike Steven Spielberg, the trial lawyer must plan his presentation like a Hollywood director. Each shot must be planned with precision and care. The trial lawyer must carefully present his evidence, be it documents, lay witnesses or expert witnesses. There are no retakes in a jury trial. The trial lawyer is allowed one chance to present their case to the jury. It should be noted that the trial lawyer is a persuader, a reasonable convincer. And unlike a salesman, he must sell his product to a panel of jurors while being chastised by the judge and interrupted by opposing counsel. This type of lawyering is the most demanding but at the same time very rewarding. In this chapter we will not only discuss the lawyer's role, but the nonattorney's role as well.

The Courtroom

Courtrooms are the epicenters of justice throughout the United States. The floor plan is very much like the law itself, for it communicates predictability and absolute authority. All who enter instinctively know their place. It is a magnificent stage deliberately designed to convey a tone of reverence and order to its occupants. The participants are both lay and professional. The most striking element of the courtroom is the floor plan itself. It separates the judge, jury, lawyers, and the gallery. The judge's chair and podium are elevated far above all others. This reflects the power and final rule of the judge. Furthermore, judges have their own door for access to the courtroom. The jury also has its own door and assigned seating, which is also elevated in order to see and hear the lawyers and witnesses with ease. Witnesses take their seat in the witness box close to the judge and a safe distance from the lawyers. The attorneys sit at separate tables in the well of the court room. Direct and cross exam take place from these tables. Attorneys must stand when addressing the court and shall speak clearly and audibly at all times.

The well is separated from the gallery by a wooden partition that extends the width the courtroom. This architectural device bars non-attorneys from entry. The gallery is composed of relatives, the press, and the public. They enter through doors at the back of the courtroom. Generally gallery members are forbidden to pass the bar without express consent of the court. Cell phones, hats, newspapers, food, drink, and gum chewing are prohibited. Speaking or other outbursts are similarly forbidden. Generally, business attire is required by all who attend. This atmosphere is appropriately one of business, hence the semiformal attire. Formality and protocol are unmistakable. It is very similar to a church; although church and court are very different entities, they are very similar in their floor plan.

There are also strict rules of decorum. Punctuality, respect, and dignity are expected from all. Punctuality, for instance, recognizes that the time of all courtroom participants has value. Tardiness is an affront to the dignity of the court. In addition, all participants must speak loudly and distinctly. This allows for a clear and accurate record to be taken by the court reporter. No nods or shakes of the head are allowed in court. Such actions are ambiguous. One must speak clearly, plainly, and unambiguously. Finally courtesy must be the guiding watchword.

This "pressure cooker" atmosphere demands lightning-like thinking by all participants. Protocol, pressure, and formality make us stronger thinkers. Casual thinking is not allowed in court. Casual behavior is certainly not. Formal thought is painful thought. Nothing great ever came from "relaxed thinking". This is a message that the courtroom floor plan sends loud and clear. Where is your formal chamber where you can engage in serious thought? Be sure to search for that dignified, orderly place where you can read, study, and think your best. Finally, when it comes to business, you can carry courtroom formality with you wherever you go. This will enable you to be the most serious person in the room. The result is that you will stand head and shoulders above the rest.

The Jury Big Brain

The "jury big brain" finds its roots in the U.S. Constitution. Whether it is a criminal issue or a civil issue, the parties to a legal dispute have a right to a jury trial by their peers. The "jury big brain" is somewhat similar to the "master-mind" concept discussed at length in the classic *Think and Grow Rich* by Napoleon Hill. (The Ralton Society 1937). The notion here is that a plaintiff or defendant is entitled to a jury of their peers when deciding liability and damages or guilt and innocence.

The constitutional framers really got this one right. Who better to evaluate trial evidence than multiple individuals with diverse ages, backgrounds and experiences? The case will now be examined by a number of human prisms. The benefit here is that multiple jurors ensure that no single piece of evidence is missed. This is essentially redundancy. With such a thorough vetting of the evidence, a fair, just, and accurate verdict is more likely. This legal "big brain" is much more powerful than a single mind. Several minds are simply stronger than a single one. The result is true diversity of thought practiced by diverse individuals essentially trapped together in the jury room until a final verdict is achieved.

The whole in this case is clearly greater than the individual parts. A jury will struggle, argue, examine, and apply the law to the evidence. The jury system is the primary building block of democracy where one's vote truly counts. A statewide or national election tends to dilute one's vote. This is not the case in a trial. Unlike the ballot box, there is no privacy in the jury room. Each voter must justify and defend their vote. This process may take hours or even days. Only through such a process can a just verdict be reached. Each juror views the evidence through their own lens of life experience, common sense, and personal observation. A single juror will typically spot a fact that all the others may have missed entirely. This redundancy ensures that no sliver of evidence is overlooked.

All of us can take advantage of this powerful tool by forming our own "jury big brain" It is a great device to solve our own problems, be they personal or business. With just two or more people to contribute, no problem is too great or too complex to solve. Your "jury" of friends or colleagues will be mentally stronger as a group than individually. Such a gathering of minds generates an exponential intelligence and energy capable of just about anything. The added bonus is that unlike the random selection of a jury panel, you can choose the members of your own "jury big brain." Although your members may be more like-minded than diverse, the advantage of group problem-solving is clear.

The key takeaway regarding the American jury system is the assembly of diverse citizens. They are commanded by law to report for jury duty. Many do not wish to serve in the first place. This reluctant assembly of total strangers constitutes a truly authentic melting pot. They are now compelled to reason together for a just result. This is authentic diversity of thought in motion. The jury members eventually reach a final verdict and usually get it right. This is a difficult process that brings together a mixture of observation and life experiences for the common goal of problem- solving.

The entire trial process compels the jury to collectively think like attorneys. The judge is "the educator in chief" in this regard. The trial judge gives extensive written and verbal instructions to the jury. They are given a crash course in the law of the present case. Jurors are instructed to follow the evidence wherever it may lead. They are ordered to discard their own passions and prejudices and focus only on law and facts. This last instruction prevents the distortion of justice by emotion and sympathy. Remember: if the facts are distorted by emotion, justice is distorted by definition. Below are some typical examples of actual jury instruction guidelines from *Minnesota Jury Instruction Guides* (2018) Eagan, Minnesota: Thomson West. In fact, they were authored and edited in part by my law school professor Mike Steenson. These instructions are designed to keep the jurors mentally on track. The judge not only orally instructs, but issues a written copy to reinforce these important instructions from *Jury Instruction Guides*:

- Of all the people in the courtroom, it is vital that you the jury be able to hear and see everything. If any of you have difficulty hearing or understanding what a witness is saying, or if a witness or an attorney should block your view, raise your hand immediately so that we can correct that.
- Here are some basic rules about your job as a juror. Your job will be to find what the facts are in this case by considering the evidence. As judge, I will apply the rules and tell you what can and cannot consider as evidence.
  - > The attorneys' questions are not evidence. The witnesses' answers are.

- You cannot consider anything you hear or learn about the case outside this courtroom. You must follow the instructions on what you can consider as evidence.
- You may take notes during the trial. You do not have to. Do not let your note taking distract you. Use your notes as an aid to your memory. Fit them in with your total recollection of the facts.
- Wait until you have heard all the evidence before you make up your mind. Your best guide is your own judgement, experience, and common sense.
- You and only you can decide the facts. Do not take anything I say or do as a sign of what the verdict should be. You must apply the law to the facts. You must follow the law I give you even if you don't agree with it.
- The goal of jury deliberations is to talk among yourselves in order to reach an agreement about the verdict. This agreement must be consistent with your own judgement. Each of you must decide the case for yourself but do so only after you have fully considered the views of your fellow jurors. Re-examine your own view and change your mind, if you decide your original view was mistaken. But do not change your mind just because other jurors disagree, or simply because of pressure to return a verdict.
- You must not allow sympathy, prejudice, or emotion to influence your verdict. The quality of your service will be reflected in the verdict you return to this court. A just and proper verdict contributes to the administration of justice.

These jury instructions are incredibly valuable, as they establish logical reasoning skills directed at problem-solving. Even the most difficult problems can be resolved with such rules. For instance, the notion of seeing and hearing everything in the courtroom is essential to absorbing all of the evidence presented. The gift of attention is never lost in the courtroom. Not all evidence presented can be considered. If the evidence is objectionable, it must be discarded. This rule is designed to encourage a singular focus on only relevant evidence. Distractions of extraneous or unduly prejudicial evidence must be eliminated in order keep that proper focus.

In line with this rule is the notion that the lawyer's question cannot stand on its own. It is probative, but not evidence. The most important part of such an exchange is the actual answer. Only the actual answer of said witness rises to the level of admissible evidence. The tone and demeanor of the witness bears on their credibility and can also be considered. For example, if the witness looks down or away from his questioner during cross examination, this may indicate deception. Difficult questions are a part of life, but not all must be answered. In the world of business, you may find an opponent's question unfair and inflammatory. Your questioner may be preparing a trap for you. One tactic is to simply respond by pointing out that the question is not evidence and will not be answered. This is one option that law students and lawyers don't have, but you do.

Also, in the interests of focus, outside research is expressly disallowed. "Googling" is forbidden. Furthermore, anything a juror may hear outside of trial shall be ignored. This promotes fairness for both the plaintiff and the defense. It would be unfair to review information that the litigants and the judge do not know about. Similarly, fellow jurors would not know of the extracurricular evidence that puts them at a disadvantage as well. Outside information can also be unreliable, unlike court-approved testimony and evidence. Scientifically speaking, the courtroom is very much like a hermetically sealed laboratory.

Such a lab seeks to avoid all outside contamination to ensure pure results. In the interests of those pure results, the judge typically instructs that attorney conduct is also not evidence. In addition the judge's own conduct cannot be considered in arriving at a verdict.

The judge will also carefully provide written law to the jurors as well. That law will contain an understandable listing of its basic elements. For instance, in a murder trial the specific elements of the crime itself will be enumerated. The offense itself must be defined. Intent, premeditation, and malice aforethought are examples of such elements. These elements must then be applied to the evidence from the trial. The judge also provides a written jury verdict form that structures the verdict itself. It consists of several questions requiring a "yes" or "no" response. During the process, jurors must endeavor to reach a consensus, while all the while relying upon their own life experiences and common sense.

Finally, sympathy, prejudice, and passion must be eliminated from the entire process. These three emotions are inherently unreliable, given their subjectivity. In order to achieve justice, logical reasoning must be exercised. The goal here is not to strip us of our own humanity, but to simply restrain our own unreliable impulses. This also compels us to apply the law, even if we don't agree with that law. The process is not cold-blooded, but rather seeks to apply cold, objective reasoning. This type of reasoning is far more likely to produce a correct result. But once again, we must not forego our humanity. One of my favorite phrases is the following: "justice tempered by mercy"-Milton. Both are advanced traits that we can all apply in life.

Jurors are typically not allowed to ask questions during the actual trial. They are required to carefully listen to all of the evidence. The trial is a form of one-way communication that compels the jurors to absorb all evidence without interruption. Thereafter, they may explode into deliberation and debate in the privacy of the jury room. Imagine the possibilities if we can apply these skills to our personal and business problems. The power of attention here is self-evident.

The added bonus is the confidence such an experience imprints upon the jurors. They have intellectually struggled over life or death, freedom or imprisonment, financial compensation or financial ruin. Only after agonizing over such momentous issues, can they walk out of that courtroom taller than when they walked in. They walk out exhausted, but equally confident.

Once again, you too can assemble your own version of a "jury big brain." It is as simple as assembling a group of your own trusted advisors, friends, and colleagues to focus on any project that you may have. This will create a muscular thinking dynamic where each can hear the views and observations of the other. Think of such an assembly of minds as a collaboration. People do it all the time in the form of book clubs, business meetings, and small group discussions. The takeaway here is that if twelve strangers, forced together in a real jury, can hash out a solution, imagine what a group of friends and colleagues can achieve. One of my favorite contractions in the English language is the term: "Let's." It is also a phrase often used by Jim Rohn, the famous business philosopher. "Let's" is simply working on a result together, rather than alone. It is collaboration in its purest form without regard as to who gets the credit.

Burdens of Proof

The trial attorney is required to prove a case within basic standards. These legal standards are known as "burdens of proof."

The burden of proof is the threshold level of persuasion necessary to win a case. These particular burdens of proof fall into three separate categories. They are reasonable doubt, clear and convincing evidence, and preponderance of evidence.

The first and most familiar standard is the "beyond a reasonable doubt" standard. It requires the state to prove its case against a criminal defendant beyond a reasonable doubt. Reasonable doubt does not mean any doubt and certainly does not mean beyond a shadow of a doubt. It simply means that if in the mind of the jurors a reasonable doubt exists as to guilt, the defendant must walk free. This standard is demandingly high as the personal liberty of the accused is at stake. The standard compels jurors to act with dispassionate reason in evaluating each piece of evidence that could reasonably find a defendant not guilty. That verdict cannot be based upon emotion. It cannot be based upon speculation. It must be based upon reason that can be detected through inference. In other words, any juror can infer a conclusion based upon facts and circumstances presented. Criminal defense lawyers typically will list as many reasonable doubts as possible, hoping that just one will let his client off the hook. The verdict must be based upon sound judgement, common sense. and the evidence proved up at trial.

Another standard of proof is the clear and convincing standard. This generally applies to a claim of punitive damages. These extra money damages are designed to punish and deter a defendant's conduct. Therefore, they must be proved at a much higher level. For instance, suppose we have a drunk driver who severely injures a pedestrian. The driver's conduct may demonstrate a reckless disregard for the rights and safety of another. Punitive damages then apply. Compensatory damages are typically for pain, suffering, lost wages, medical bills, and lost profits that a plaintiff incurs in the past and will incur in the future. Exemplary damages can be awarded in addition to compensatory damages. Since they are not actual damages, the greater burden of proof applies.

The final burden of proof is the "preponderance of evidence" standard. This standard is the lowest of the standards and only requires the plaintiff to prove that it is more likely than not that his version of the facts is accurate and that he should recover. If the plaintiff proves his case 51 percent versus the defendant's case of 49 percent on any given issue, the plaintiff prevails. "51 percent" is defined as more likely than not. This burden of proof is applicable to a civil trial where one party seeks money damages against another.

These exacting standards can be applied by all of us in attempting to prove our own arguments. In life's circumstances, these standards can be gently applied to persuade your own audience. Of course, these standards are situational and will be dependent upon the formality of your situation. With the possible exception of the reasonable doubt standard, life does not require scientific test tube precision. Precise thinking is valuable, but in the ordinary course of ordinary lives, the standards are lower. Most matters cannot be proved with test tube precision. Life always gives us some margin of error, so we must take advantage of it.

Reasonable doubts are also important because they are the identifiable things that we can lose on. These are the issues that find you at your weakest. Reasonable doubt standards identify those weaknesses. This particular standard allows you to hit the most difficult issues head on and hopefully eliminate them. In business, your opponents may seek to exploit your "doubts." Reasonable doubts make one more realistic. It is important to realize your own reasonable doubts in life. Avoid unreasonable worry about things that statistically will never happen. Your worries in life must be within reason and must be confronted head on.

You will always have an opponent raising doubts against you. These particular reasonable doubts are a two-edged sword. They are cannon fodder for your opponents, but they are also weaknesses, that if timely addressed, make you stronger. The rule here is to eliminate the doubts and then move on. Dispose of the issues and get on with life. Any prosecutor that has completed his trial and can say to himself, "I have eliminated all reasonable doubts",can rest well, knowing that he will obtain the desired verdict.

The defense lawyer raises any possible doubt and attempts to translate it to reasonable doubt. When it comes to worry, we must identify only the reasonable doubts or worries in life. The reasonable doubts that statistically can happen are what are relevant. Try not to apply a "beyond any doubt standard" in life because statistically it is not going to happen and leads to needless worry. This is essentially "focused thinking" on what matters.

Don't fall prey to the attempts of the "defense attorneys" in your life who employ unreasonable doubt standards. They try to make you exercise mental gymnastics to agree with their point of view. The path of least resistance in our thinking is usually and statistically the correct one. As George Berger once stated, "What was probable, probably happened." Berger furthermore characterized this rule as a yardstick for testing the credibility of evidence or any argument, for that matter. If you must engage in mental gymnastics in order to buy the argument of your opponent, then you are going down the wrong path. The path of least resistance regarding the most likely probability is usually the correct one. In essence, it is better to adopt the simplest theory versus an outrageously complex one. Remember Occam's Razor: "The simplest explanation is usually the correct one." Embrace the simple. Embrace the rule of probability.

Evidentiary Standards

Trials and trial lawyers are regulated by a number of evidentiary rules. This section will cover the most basic of these rules that control every single piece of evidence that comes before a jury. The rules of evidence are sensitive to two basic concepts: time considerations and relevancy considerations. These two concepts go hand in hand. The idea here is that trials are limited in their scope as well as their duration. These rules filter vast amounts of evidence into a distilled, pure product. A trial lawyer must compress years of fact gathering into several days or weeks. She must focus on the most important issues and avoid the immaterial. Exhibits and testimony must be reasonably calculated to lead to relevant evidence. The Federal Rules of Evidence are particularly instructive:

Rule 401. Definition of Relevant Evidence

> "Relevant evidence" means evidence having any tendency to make the existence of any fact that is of consequence to the determination of the action more probable or less probable than it would be without the evidence.

This is a classic example of legal jargon. Don't be intimidated. This rule requires that at trial, we employ a singular focus on only the essential. We employ laser-like attention on matters of consequence that determine issues. No extraneous evidence on collateral issues is allowed. It keeps the lawyer's and jury's eyes on target. Relevant evidence keeps us focused on what matters and prevents jury contamination.

For instance, if a plaintiff is bringing a claim for his own injuries, the fact that his wife brought a lawsuit years earlier for her injuries, is not relevant. Her claim is immaterial even though she has followed a similar path in court. Similarities do not necessarily equate to relevancy. Furthermore, the probative value of such evidence must outweigh the likelihood of unfair prejudice. If her claim were admitted into evidence, the implication would be that litigiousness runs in families. This would be unfairly prejudicial to her husband's case.

In our daily lives, as well as in business, it is important to focus on the important and the relevant. The most common violation of this rule is TMI, or "Too Much Information." The notion here is to avoid drowning your listener in unlimited information. Initially, this may give one a sense of completion or a sense of "nothing missed." This temptation must be resisted. Life is short. The jury trial is even shorter. Trial lawyers focus on the important and the germane during a limited trial window. Violation of this rule will invite harsh rulings from the judges in court as well as in our own lives. Those judges can be friends, employers, co-employees, or our customers. People today simply do not have time for all the possible information that could be remotely connected to every possible issue.

The rule of relevant evidence demands that we stay on message in regard to our presentation of facts and arguments. Relevancy respects the time of others. I am reminded of a judge who once said to me, "Mr. Cody, get to the point. If there is one." This rule of evidence separates the important from the unimportant, and the relevant from the immaterial. This is why Vince Lombardi stated to his players on more than one occasion, "Discard the immaterial." Once we have discarded the immaterial in our lives, the focus is finally clear and uncluttered. Think of it as the fine art of brevity or a truly great "elevator speech."

Causation

Another advanced legal concept utilized by trial lawyers is the concept of causation, defined by U.S. Legal.com as follows:

"Causation is the relationship of cause and effect of an act or omission and damages alleged in a tort or personal injury action."

This definition essentially means that an attorney must prove that any damages are directly, substantially, or proximately caused by the actions of another. It is essentially a "but-for" argument: were it not for the conduct of the defendant, the injury would not have occurred. Typically, this applies to negligent conduct of a defendant. For instance, if a defendant driver does not maintain proper lookout, speed, and control of the vehicle, and then causes an accident, the defendant is held to have legally caused the accident. However, the cause of the plaintiff's injuries will be an entirely separate matter determined by medical experts. Defense lawyers are always looking for a fact that can break the chain of medical causation. Prior medical treatment for a similar injury is a classic example.

Another example of causation addresses the criminal law concept of chain of custody. If a murder weapon is to be introduced into evidence, the prosecution must prove that the police had continuous and uninterrupted custody of the murder weapon. This extends from the crime scene all the way to the courtroom several months or years later. The rule ensures the integrity of that evidence. It guarantees that the evidence has not been tampered with or switched. If the chain of custody is interrupted in any way, that evidence may be excluded. If we circle back to the personal injury trial, one must prove uninterrupted causation between the client's injuries in an accident to the date of trial. If a client has a second injury between injury number one and the trial date, this can effectively break the chain of causation regarding the plaintiff's injuries. As you analyze any cause and effect problem, be on guard against "causation breakers."

It is important to note what causation is not. Causation is not chronology. Sequence alone is not enough to meet the standard of causation. By this we mean that if event A occurs and subsequently event B occurs shortly after, this does not necessarily mean that event A produced event B. There must be an inciting producer of the second event. For instance, if a plaintiff receives a vaccination and almost immediately develops an injurious side effect, the closeness in time itself, does not necessary prove cause. In this instance, outside expert medical opinion is required to connect the two events. An expert opinion must show how and why the injury was produced by the vaccination. This is known as the mechanism of injury.

From a practical standpoint, we must martial all researched evidence to be sure we have met our burden of causation. This is not casual thinking. It is causal thinking. Just because two events occur close together in time, it does not mean they are connected. Conversely, even though a cause and effect are separated by a significant time gap, there can still be a causal relationship. Once again, like a chain of evidence, we must analyze each link in the chain in order to successfully connect two separate events. These links in the chain are the "hows and whys" of causation.

The concept of causation is a valuable one in day to day analysis of problems. It forces one to analyze two or more events and determine whether they are related or simply sequential. It helps us see things for what they really are. Causation clarifies and captures the real issues at hand. It truly helps us connect evidence and events in life. It can also tell us why the event happened in the first place.

An offshoot of the concept is origin and cause. For instance, in the typical arson case where a building has burned to the ground, the fire department and the insurance company will conduct their investigation of the blaze. The investigation will focus on two things. The first is where the fire began geographically. This addresses where in the structure the blaze started. The cause addresses what started the fire in the first place. For example: was it an electrical short in wiring or a match with an accelerant? Finally, the tool of causation demands that things happen for a provable and scientific reason. Never let anyone tell you that some terrible event was a "freak occurrence." This is lazy thinking! Truly freak occurrences are actually quite rare. There is almost always some type of human cause or "pilot error" at work.

Hearsay

Hearsay is an additional courtroom concept that is probably the most well-known evidentiary rule. Hearsay is the legal term that describes statements made outside of court not subject to cross examination. Most evidentiary codes defining hearsay adopt verbatim the rule as expressed in the Federal Rules of Evidence. Rule 801 states as follows:

> Hearsay means a statement that: 1) the declarant does not make while testifying at the current trial or hearing; and 2) a party offers in evidence to prove the truth of the matter asserted in the statement.

The main thrust of hearsay for our purposes is this: secondhand witnesses are not reliable. Secondhand statements cannot be admitted in court as a matter of fairness. If the author of the secondhand statement is not available in court, the opposing lawyer cannot cross examine that particular person as they are absent. All witnesses are subject to rigorous direct and cross examination. To allow hearsay disrupts this rule. Hearsay is unreliable because by its own definition it cannot be subjected to meaningful cross examination. For instance, a document, even if signed by its creator, cannot itself be cross-examined. That document must be accompanied by its author who can explain various details of the hows and whys as to its origin. Obtaining information straight from the witness first hand is the most reliable method. Firsthand information is best. The rule also allows the jury to evaluate the appearance and manner of the witness. This directly impacts the credibility or believability of the witness.

The lesson here is that we must assert not only in argument ,but in analysis, our own direct facts and not someone else's. Credible people don't say "I heard from a friend who heard it from a friend." Secondhand information is as dangerous as gossip. It is unreliable because the information has been twice removed and cannot be vetted for its truthfulness and accuracy. The hearsay rule encourages facts coming directly from the declarant. Without the hearsay rule, our facts become distorted the further it is removed from the original declarant. Accuracy is the goal of any hearsay rule. Accuracy is the foundation of truth.

Direct Evidence and Circumstantial Evidence

Another evidentiary rule concerns direct evidence versus circumstantial evidence. Direct evidence is something that the witness can perceive through one or more of the five senses. It is therefore reliable, subject to cross examination of course. For instance, external forces can obstruct one of the witnesses' five senses and therefore they are open to impeachment or challenge under cross examination. In contrast, circumstantial evidence is a number of evidentiary facts that lead to an inescapable conclusion. In most courts, direct evidence is on an equal playing field with circumstantial evidence. Both are equally acceptable to a jury for their evaluation. One is not necessarily better than the other.

We must first look for direct evidence to properly assess a situation. For instance, if we see something or hear something with our own eyes and ears, this is reliable sensory input. However, we cannot allow our own emotions to distort this very input. We must be aware of obstructions to our own five senses. They can be heavily influenced by external conditions such as lighting, audio distractions, unreliable memory, excitement, and our own inattention. The goal here is to see and hear things as they truly are. One must evaluate evidence without prejudices distorting them. Life experiences and knowledge can certainly be used to clarify and filter that input but actual prejudice must be avoided.

Circumstantial evidence requires a higher degree of effort. It points indirectly at a conclusion. It requires us to string together existing facts and evidence and reach a logical conclusion. In essence, the facts added together construct a whole. We draw conclusions from the circumstances that were observed, even though there is not one witness who saw it happen at the time. Not unlike an airplane crash, we piece together the destroyed parts of a plane to reach a conclusion as to why and how the crash occurred. This is essentially a legal puzzle assembled piece by piece to tell the whole story.

Negligence

Negligence can be defined as the failure to exercise prudent conduct that a reasonable person would employ under like circumstances. The elements of negligence are duty, breach of duty, causation, and damages. The reasonable prudent person standard demands that we not be neglectful in our behavior. Negligence requires an exercise of due care in all matters at all times. This is a duty we owe to others. It is as simple as a rear end car crash. Negligence is a legal term for neglect. If someone is not paying attention and because of that inattention causes a car crash, they have breached that duty of care. They will now be held accountable via the device known as a lawsuit.

Practically and legally, neglect has a great cost. It has severe consequences. Neglect causes injury. The failure to be prudent and attentive causes all of us to pay a high price. In order to avoid paying this high price, one must maintain sound habits rather than neglectful ones. The law demands that every person act prudently. If they fail in that prudence, this is neglectful or negligent conduct. Once again, it is as simple as keeping proper lookout, speed, and control of our motor vehicle on a highway. The high price of even the smallest amount of inattention can be injury or death, not to mention the monetary costs of a lawsuit. The reasonable, prudent business person does not allow carelessness to infect their daily habits. They thereby avoid carelessness itself. Make note that this not intentional or deliberate conduct. It is a simple failure of mindfulness and situational awareness.

One of my favorite legal concepts is the doctrine of comparative fault. I favor it because it demands personal accountability of both parties to a lawsuit. The judge will properly require the jury to apportion the fault of the plaintiff and the defendant on a percentage basis. For instance, if a collision occurs at an intersection where the defendant runs a red light, then the negligent driver pays one hundred percent of plaintiff's damages. However, if the facts are altered just a bit (here comes the law school hypothetical) and plaintiff was speeding, this will change the whole dynamic. For instance, plaintiff may now be twenty percent at fault. The result is that the plaintiff's own negligence reduces his money damages by that same twenty percent.

The law of comparative negligence is brilliant. The rule not only penalizes neglect, but recognizes that in most cases both parties are responsible for some fault. After all, nobody's perfect. This is essentially court mandated personal responsibility. The most reasonably prudent person prevails in the end. This is a great rule of law and life.

It accurately distributes legal responsibility to both parties, which is the essence of justice itself. The notion of comparative fault illustrates a great life lesson. This lesson states that everyone must share in personal responsibility. No one gets off the hook in the legal system, no matter how sympathetic their plight may be. Each litigant's contributory actions and behavior will be judged. And further, those actions will be either rewarded or punished. This is the essence of personal accountability and is legally recognized as such.

On the opposite end of the spectrum, it is important to realize that people tend to follow patterns of carelessness. They usually have a number of negligent mishaps in their lives. People tend to follow a pattern of repeated negligence. This repeated neglect adds up, which is why we call it cumulative. It adds up over time until disaster occurs. For instance, car accidents are usually a result of a driving lifetime of cumulative neglect. It first starts with rolling through a stop sign, then failing to signal, then driving while using a cell phone until finally disaster in the form of a severe motor vehicle crash.

The high cost of such neglect comes in the form of higher insurance rates, and a money judgment against the negligent driver for damages. In essence, this is a metaphor for life. We cannot be neglectful in the details of our lives. Even the smallest details, such as flipping a turn signal, if failed upon, can cause tragic results. The moral of the story is this: do not neglect even the smallest thing in life because neglect can be a habit. It happens over time. The law of negligence requires us to continuously pay attention to the details of our surroundings. This is simple situational awareness. It requires us to pick up on life's signals. Some signals are subtle and some are more obvious. Prudent conduct is fueled by the twin engines of situational awareness and focus.

Facts, Opinions, Predictions and Persuasions

These next four notions are practical considerations for the courtroom as well as business. Their definitions as well as their distinctions are critical to effective argument. Consider them the "Four Horseman of Reasonable Argument." Facts are the first of these concepts . Facts are cold, accurate, and generally immutable. They are backed up by diverse, reliable authorities. They are also known for their consistency and authenticity. Truly pure facts are also undisputed and may be agreed to by both parties. Facts ,however, can be disputed. This requires a finder of fact to determine the most persuasive version, based on consistencies and inconsistencies in the storyline. The finder can be a judge, jury, or other ultimate decision maker.

Remember: "Your feelings aren't facts." (Laura Schlessinger). It is imperative to avoid confusion between the two. We all have feelings and that's okay. Passion can be a great thing when properly directed. Simply be sure that you restrain those passions with logic. Don't argue your feelings. Argue your facts! This logic- driven braking system is as effective in the business world as it is in the courtroom.

The second horseman is opinion, a viewpoint researched or not, leading to a conclusion by the declarant. It is a belief or view based on some facts or even feelings. This view can equally rely on no facts at all. Emotion can be a key element of the opinion as well. Financial motive can also put a spin on the facts. For instance, at trial, expert witnesses are typically paid by each party in order to provide the jury with assistance in interpreting complex evidence and facts. Their expertise in engineering, medicine, science, or accounting can by invaluable to the finders of fact. Expert opinion is superior to mere amateur opinion in most all cases. Remember, anyone can have an opinion.

Predictions are the third horseman. Predictions direct themselves at potential events that have not yet occurred. The prediction may occur tomorrow, next week or may never happen at all. Predictions, like opinions, may be based upon fact or feelings. Watch for predictions that are based on statistical patterns of behavior or conduct. They are, as a general proposition, reliable.

The final horseman in our quartet directs itself at persuasions. Persuasion is the fine art of shaping and blending the first three horsemen. This is a deliberate process, which can result in the combining of opinions, facts and predictions to appear as outright truth. This process, when properly employed, can provide a jury with a clean, helpful, final argument. But if abused, it can only serve to mislead.

The courtroom lawyer, effectively combines the above four horsemen of reasonable argument to persuade the jury. Facts, opinions, predictions, and persuasions can be applied in many settings both business and personal. A blend of all four can make your pitch that much more effective and persuasive. But remember to manage the subtle differences between the four.

A last point regarding trial advocacy deals with final argument. The closing argument is essentially a speech given to the jury after all of the evidence is admitted. The final summation before the jury is not evidence in and of itself. Only the testimony and the admitted exhibits rise to the level of evidence. This final summation ties together the evidence and the attorney's theory of the case. Evidence cannot exist in a vacuum, so the attorneys summarize the evidence as they see it with all legitimate inferences that can be reasonably drawn. The goal is to explain with evidence why a litigant should win. It is often a very helpful tool to help the jury to remember and to organize the facts presented during a lengthy trial.

Hypothetical Questions

I find that the hypothetical fact question to be irritating and equally unhelpful. It is rampant in news interviews and cocktail hour discussions. As discussed above, hypotheticals were a necessary evil in the law school classroom. At one time they served as great illustrators of law and its necessary application to imaginary fact patterns. Exam questions were dependent upon them. However, in the real world of facts, hypotheticals can be quite useless and downright annoying. My advice would be to refuse to answer any "hypo" unless absolutely necessary. Remember, most hypos simply pop into the amateur questioner's head with absolutely no prior research.

I remember using this hypo avoidance tactic myself in court. It involved a summary judgement motion where both parties stipulated to a set of facts. The only thing left for decision was the judge's application of the law to facts. During oral argument, the judge attempted to change the agreed upon facts via a hypothetical question. He essentially stated; "What if these new facts applied? What if such and such actually occurred?" I answered that my client has enough real case facts to deal with without imaginary ones. I sidestepped the court's question. The judge let me be. It was a bit of a gamble, but I did win the motion.

Keep in mind that there are various tip offs to an incoming hypothetical. Look for the question with the following preface: may, might, can, could, would, suppose, and of course, "what if." If you encounter any of these words, this is a sure sign of a hypothetical trap. Think of it this way: hypotheticals assert events that have never happened. Based on this absence alone, statistically, they are not likely to occur in the future. So what's the point? In the end, there is nothing to be gained by answering such a question. By this, I mean that you will never satisfy the questioner no matter what your answer may be. Above all else, you should recognize that the hypo is nothing but a pitfall. Simply tell your questioner that you do not engage in hypotheticals as a rule. Rise above the circumstances. As Rooster Cogburn once said, "I do not abide hypotheticals. I find the real-world vexing enough." (*True Grit*—Paramount Pictures 2010).

BLACK LETTER LAW

- If the facts are distorted by emotion, justice is distorted by definition.
- Questions are probative but they are not evidence in and of themselves.
- Not every question deserves an answer.
- Form your own "jury big brain." It promotes true diversity of thought.
- Be logical. Be human. This is "justice tempered by mercy"-Milton
- The courtroom conveys the ultimate design for order and decorum.
- Jury instruction guidelines are a great resource for collective problem solving.
- Focus on only relevant evidence in life and in business. "Discard the immaterial." -Vince Lombardi
- Remember Occam's Razor: "All things being equal, the simplest explanation is usually the correct one." Avoid mental gymnastics.
- Causation is a producer of an event. It is not chronology.
- Second-hand witnesses and out of court statements are not reliable. Watch out for hearsay.
- Circumstantial evidence can be just as reliable as direct evidence.
- When it comes to negligence, comparative fault demands personal responsibility of both parties to a lawsuit.
- The reasonable, prudent person is not guilty of carelessness.

- "Your feelings are not facts".-Laura Schlessinger
- Be sure to understand the difference between facts, opinions, predictions, and persuasions. These are the Four Horsemen of reasonable argument.
- Do not abide hypothetical questions.

CHAPTER 4

Veteran Attorney Thinking

This next chapter offers the toolbox of mental skills only possessed by the mature lawyer, who has survived the early years of inexperience to now claim the battle-hardened mantle of a seasoned lawyer. To quote Louis Nizer, My Life in Court, (Doubleday 1961, p. 159):

> A client, particularly in a matrimonial controversy, is so emotionally involved that he cannot be trusted to have cool judgment. His lawyer must be firm and in full control of the case, or he disserves his client. The lawyer must not be dependent on his client's favor, either because of fees or even friendship. What a man in legal trouble needs is not merely a friend, but a counselor. If a client is strongly guided by skillful and loyal hands, he has received also the most significant expression of friendship. Sentiment alone will not do. When a lawyer, in order to please the client, permits him to have his way, he may incur his favor temporarily, but they're both likely to be in trouble at the end…I have then used my skills to obtain the most modest but appropriate terms, and guided him to a solution, which never became part of a blazing court drama.

Mr. Nizer aptly makes the point with repeated references to skills. The point of this chapter is to elaborate on this toolbox of mature legal skills. A veteran lawyer successfully utilizes them during the representation of each client. The most important of these are listed below.

a. Negotiation Skills

Lawyers are by necessity skilled negotiators. At every stage of a lawsuit, settlement is always an option. An out of court settlement eliminates the risks of an expensive trial altogether. Opposing lawyers privately attempt to settle their differences between each other. They may also do so at a mediation with a professional mediator. In many cases, mediation is mandated by the court. They may also be pressured by a judge to negotiate a settlement to avoid a trial. An attorney will sometimes go in high, and the other side will go in low, and an accommodation is reached somewhere in between. When an attorney proffers an opening demand, it is within reason and predicts the best result in court.

When attorneys mediate their case, a mediator will shuttle from room to room where the two parties are sequestered. He will convey offers, ideas, pros, and cons of both sides. All things are negotiable! Typically, a mediator will tell the party in each room how bad their case is. The downside of their case will be explained in detail. This method reflects the mediator's attempt to soften up each side so that they become more realistic. Mediators employ Dr. Phil's tactic of "getting real" about unpleasant realities. After hours of negotiation, eventually a settlement can be reached by the use of this tactic. The mediator is neutral and can never be called as a witness. His notes can never be subpoenaed. This encourages both parties to be frank with their mediator. Most mediators will tell you that the mark of a good settlement is a settlement that neither party is happy with.

One type of negotiation strategy can be drawn from the mediator's toolbox of skills and used in your own negotiations. These negotiations may involve your own customers. One tactic would be to truthfully explain the pros *and* cons of your product or service. This strategy promotes complete candor with whomever you are dealing. By acknowledging our weaknesses as well as our strengths, we gain a greater degree of credibility in the eyes of our customer. Our customers can and will detect those weaknesses at some point in time anyway. Honesty in the beginning can bear great fruit later in the form of referrals and a solid business reputation.

The brutal honesty employed in legal mediations can assist one in achieving a fair resolution. Negotiation is a trading forum wherein one party trades something of value to another who has something of value as well. But do not forget that negotiation is an adverse process in a somewhat cooperative atmosphere. Each side has competing interests and goals that contradict the other side. Never forget the use of leverage in negotiation. You may have a fact or selling point that you can use to leverage your position. Remember: levers move things. Leverage moves people. This leverage gives lawyers a strength, not unlike a fulcrum, which they would not have otherwise. Lawyers may use a prior injury, a criminal conviction or prior lawsuit to leverage his position and obtain a more favorable monetary settlement. It's important that we all look to various levers that will magnify our strengths to our advantage. One small fact, properly leveraged, can move mountains.

I would be remiss if I did not address something known as the "phantom offer." This refers to a hypothetical offer and is typically employed by a mediator as a way to settle the case. It goes something like this: "If I persuade the other side to offer $100,000, would your client accept it?" At first glance, this presents as a very tempting, harmless proposal. After all, we are all trying to resolve the negotiation. The true intent, however, is to discover the bottom line of one party without actually making a firm and binding offer. It is a mythical offer, which may or may not become a reality. If you answer "yes" to the hypothetical $100,000 offer, you have tipped your hand needlessly. The firm offer will certainly come back in a far lesser amount, for instance: $70,000. The lesson here is this: let no one get into your head rent free. Make it a strict rule that you will respond to firm offers only. Never get burned by a phantom offer wrapped in a hypothetical. This will get you the respect of the mediator and more importantly, your opponent.

b. Time Management Skills

A vital skill that any veteran lawyer must possess is that of time management. A major pillar of time management is "immediate doing." This means performing the necessary functions and tasks while they are still fresh in one's mind. At this point the emotion is still high and the energy is still palpable. For instance, many an inexperienced lawyer will request what is known as a "continuance." This is an attorney's request for a postponement of a scheduled motion or even trial. It typically is an indicator of poor time management or incomplete preparation, also known as "my legal secretary ate my homework." Ordinarily, trial judges will allow one and only one continuance, if any. If you catch yourself postponing something more than once, stop yourself in your own tracks. In your mind, say to yourself "motion for continuance is denied." This stops procrastination in its tracks. You must move your own life along on the court calendar. In essence, time management must be timely.

Another time management tool that is applied to lawyers is the statute of limitations. This is also known as SOL, and we all know what this means. Essentially though, these terms are identical. If a lawyer runs afoul of the statute of limitations, she will be sued for malpractice. This is essentially missing a deadline in which to bring a claim, thereby forfeiting the client's right to bring a lawsuit. One purpose of the statute of limitations is to prevent a case from getting stale. As time goes on, memories fade, witnesses disappear, and evidence cannot be found. In the lawyer's world things must be done with all deliberate speed. Deadlines are good. They move life and business along. Deadlines compel us to do what we otherwise would not do for ourselves. Finally, they require us to produce measurable results within a reasonable period of time.

When it comes to any business negotiation, be sure to determine if there is any applicable expiration date. Offers never remain open forever. At some point they are withdrawn if not accepted. Either party can place a time limit on their offer in order to pressure their opponent.

Time management and SOLs convey great life lessons for the rest of us. Do not let things wait, for waiting is the enemy of progress. Procrastination and stagnancy go hand in hand. In sum, deadlines and punishment for running afoul of deadlines are a good thing. They keeps us on track. They disposes of the matter so you can mentally move on to the next challenge. As professor Steenson said: "Dispose of the issue!" This means identify the issue, take a position, analyze it, and then finally move on.

For example, if there is a sales lead that comes to your attention, it is critical that you jump on it with all due immediacy and urgency. If one's pursuit of a business opportunity is delayed, it may very well be scooped up by your competitor. Immediate return of phone calls is another example. The unreturned phone call can be the death of all of us. The delayed return phone call is just as nefarious. This is one of the most common complaints about lawyers: unreturned phone calls. It is something that all of us, lay people and lawyers, can work on. A promptly returned phone call can put out a small grass fire, thereby preventing it from growing into a raging inferno.

Another example can occur in a typical sales meeting. If the emotion is high during a meeting with a prospect, continue the meeting. Do not let the meeting end until the issues are resolved and the sales prospect is signed up. "Sales interruptus" can kill a deal before it even begins. It is important to continue on and finish what you have started in a timely fashion. No unfinished jobs with your name on it. Finish everything.

c. Analytical Skills: The Duty to Read

The seasoned lawyer has mastered the fine art of reading and writing in the legal field. In the legal world there is nothing casual about reading and writing. Both are done with great formality and purpose. Bishop Fulton Sheen often said: "The large print giveth and the small print taketh away." The lawyer must apply "fine print" reading skills in all aspects of their practice. Legal decisions, statutes, and rules are quite technical and require great attention. A good lawyer reads a decision, an insurance policy, or a statute at least three times to properly absorb the thrust of the particular concept. If repetition is the mother of skill, the lawyer's repeated review of the same record will garner a thorough understanding of said document. It will, in effect, become part of him. The goal is to completely and totally absorb the written word and all of its nuances. This method mows down facts and details so that not a single unanalyzed sentence remains standing. In addition, the lawyer comes heavily armed with a yellow highlighter, a red pen, and post it flags. These tools reinforce "active reading" and discourage "passive reading." Finally, the seasoned lawyer will always "parse the statement." This entails a thorough breakdown of each word in a sentence and each sentence in a paragraph to discover its meaning as whole.

We can all learn from such a rigorous reading style. We need look no further than our own insurance policy, automobile owner's manual, or even the operating manual to our coffee maker. These manuals give us the basis for understanding how a thing or process works. Manufacturers of such products expect you to know all of the nuances of the product you have just purchased *before* you use it. The duty to read and the expectation of knowledge are critical for success in life. Never let it be said: "I didn't know" or "I didn't read" the proper documents beforehand. As you will see below, fine print reading skills are crucial to understanding the thought that is being conveyed via the written word.

Fine print reading skills require a precise knowledge of key phrases. Typical legal "buzz phrases" to watch out for are as follows:

1. And/or
2. Notwithstanding
3. May/shall
4. Must/may
5. Permissive/compulsory
6. Exclusion/inclusion
7. Necessary/sufficient
8. Mandatory/optional
9. Reasonable and necessary

The entire intent of the document can hinge on these connecting phrases and adjectives. Know them well. These nuances can make or break your case. As you can now see, the written word is permanent and unforgiving. Parsing and diagraming each sentence is encouraged.

Knowledge of the above terms are critical to analytical reading. Some words offer options. Others offer no escape. One must know the difference between these various terms. Typically lawyers look at elements of various legal concepts. For example, definitions of various crimes such as murder or burglary typically use and/or as the conjunctive or disjunctive requirements for said elements. If it is an "or" proposition, one or the other element will do. If "and" is indicated, then one or more elements must be added together in total to be determinative. For instance, first degree murder may require intent *and* premeditation. If both elements are not present, the definition of murder is not proven beyond a reasonable doubt and the defendant walks free.

The homeowners insurance policy is yet another example of critical word usage. These particular policies are full of legal buzz words. The most important are exclusions. This is a "Swiss cheese mentality" that insurers employ in the contracts that you are required to sign for coverage. Typically insurance contracts are contracts of adhesion, which means that the insurance company writes the language of the contract and the customer is not allowed to negotiate that language.

The Swiss cheese effect of exclusions means there are many "holes" that allow the insurance company to escape coverage, and therefore legal responsibility, for a claim. For example, if a driver intentionally runs down a pedestrian, no insurance coverage will apply to protect the driver from the claims of the injured pedestrian. This is known as an "intentional act exclusion." One must always be aware of "exclusionary" language in any contract, policy, or document. This can prevent misunderstandings from the beginning, so they will not occur later. The lesson here is quite obvious. We all have a duty to read and to read actively and thoroughly, particularly before signing. One must fully understand the import of the written word, phrase, or paragraph.

Attorneys must be masters at reading and identifying the nuances of the above terms. A simple "and" or a simple "or" can greatly change the whole dynamic of the intent of a contract or a legal document. In a sense, it requires us as readers to parse the statement, sentence, or paragraph under consideration. This is a typical trait involved in statutory construction. This is the analysis of state and federal statutes.

Another critical set of terms revolves around adjectives. Always be on the lookout for any type of adjective. Adjectives are descriptive terms that really are pregnant with opinions. They are not necessarily facts, but simply a very subjective description. Adjectives in essence are a one-word opinion that seeks to describe a certain person, place, thing, or event. It is important to be able to distinguish facts from opinions. Facts are logical. Opinions can be fraught with emotion. Always be aware of opinions which masquerade as facts. Facts are consistent and reproducible. Opinions are like mercury and just as difficult to put your thumb on.

Another analytical tool involves timelines and flow charts. Timelines are a favorite of lawyers. Timelines and flow charts allow one to make sense of complex fact situations that have occurred over months or years. Timelines manage vast amounts of information and events and distill them to a readable, understandable synopsis. People need order in most things and chronological order is the best of them all. It forces the mind to consolidate a myriad of facts into a common sense flow, which facilitates understanding. In essence, it makes the complex linear and simple.

For instance, if there are a number of parties and a number of dates, these can be distilled into a flow chart with arrows essentially connecting the dots between persons and events. Diagramming out the problem makes the problem itself much more readable and understandable. Timelines are a cold, hard analytical tool that enables one to get to the heart of the problem without distractions. The diagram allows us to see visually the flow of events between the major players in a case.

There can be various timelines, even regarding an individual's life. A personal injury case serves as an easy example for timelines. A timeline can cover a plaintiff's employment history from day one to the present. Another separate timeline can cover their medical history from day one to the present. The employment history is fairly clear-cut in that it involves dates of employment, duties of employment, the name of the employer, reason for termination, as well as any black marks or commendations in the personnel file.

A medical record chronology is a bit different. This involves any and all injuries a claimant has sustained with the treating doctors for each injury, the dates of treatments, surgeries, disability ratings, and permanent injury opinions. The medical timeline clarifies and crystalizes the entire history of an individual. A timeline can assist a jury or a judge in determining if the current claimed injury is the culprit, and if so, allow damages. The timeline can also disclose so many prior injuries, that the claim is denied. Although chronology is not necessarily causation, it is a very useful birds-eye view of the entire geography of the plaintiff's life. Cases can rise and fall on a mere timeline.

A final word on the duty to read deserves mention. When analyzing any important document or book, go immediately to the table of contents and then the conclusion. Read both first. The value of this is to prepare your mindset for the substantive reading ahead. Foreknowledge of the conclusion will prejudice you positively toward full understanding of the author's message and philosophy as you digest the material. This mental preparation will lead you to a much deeper understanding, as you already know where the author is headed.

d. Verbal and Nonverbal Communication Skills

Veteran lawyers employ precision verbal skills. They are quite precise in their own diction. Lawyers also rely on the interpretation of body language as part of their communication skills. Throughout this book we attempt to encourage you to think like a lawyer. We also encourage you to read like a lawyer. However, when it comes to body language, it is preferable not to be read like a book. Attorneys during depositions are particularly sensitive to this rule. Witnesses find it very difficult to read true intent. This is how lawyers want it. It gives them an advantage and leverage over the witness. Lawyers do not want a witness inside their head, nor do they want opposing counsel in their head as well. A granite disposition is critical to mask any feelings or emotions the lawyer may have.

The rule here is as follows: An open book is a great thing, but don't be one yourself. In life's business transactions make it your mission to be simply this: impossible to read. This air of mystery can be quite unnerving to your business opponents. A good lawyer is very reluctant to give any advantage to his opponent, or for that matter to the jury, about how he or she truly feels about a ruling, about a sudden development in the case, or an unanticipated answer to a question. They don't hang their heads in defeat. They don't shake their heads with negativity. They never appear to be dazzled or astonished. The lawyer will simply move on to the next question or issue as if nothing happened. Experienced lawyers neutralize their own body language to great effect.

The deposition is particularly instructive as to nonverbal communication skills. The deposition is a question and answer session where a witness is required to give testimony over a number of hours. A lawyer will not only elicit verbal responses from the witness, but he will also size up the witness's body language. The witness may say one thing but their body may be saying quite another. Rapid blinking, throat clearing, eye contact avoidance, touching one's face in a soothing manner may all be signals of deception. The body language essentially contradicts the verbal language. Both are closely monitored by a lawyer and his questioning is adjusted accordingly.

In a jury trial setting the attorney must engage in a whole new level of communication. Aside from a brief question Q/A session with the jurors before the trial begins, the lawyer throughout the trial is on a one-way street when it comes to communication with the jury. That one-way street is spoken communication. The lawyer speaks to the jury via opening statement, questions of witnesses, objections to evidence, and finally closing argument. Rarely is the jury allowed to ask questions. They must remain silent and absorb all the information presented. The lawyer receives no feedback except for nonverbal cues from the jury. He may adjust his tactics to accommodate his own observations of jury body language. A juror may roll his or her eyes, cross their arms, coldly stare, or shake their heads. All of these nonverbal cues must be factored in to the lawyer's overall strategy.

Not unlike an NFL coach, he must make crucial adjustments at half time in order to win at trial. A trial lawyer has the most difficult sales job of all, with no verbal feedback whatsoever. To compensate for this, they must anticipate every possible argument and question that a juror may have. Communication must be impeccable. Language must be distinct and precise. If the lawyer is vague or uncertain, he will lose the attention and faith of the jury. He must stay on message with his theory of the case, despite admonitions of the judge and objections by his opponent.

Attorneys must craft a precise delivery of clear terminology in order to effectively get their point across. There is no room for ambiguity when it comes to a lawyer's verbal skills. A lawyer's verbal skills require absolute clarity in communication. In many ways a lawyer is given just one opportunity to prove his point. Once the idea is communicated, there are no second takes, no do-overs.

e. Persuasive Skills/ Direct and Cross Examination Skills

An attorney must not only persuade a jury, but must persuade a judge as well as his client. A client may have an entirely different view of how a case should proceed, and a lawyer must effectively reign in his client via persuasion. Persuasion may effectively be applied at the very beginning of the case. In essence, the lawyer may have to talk his own client "off the ledge" and compel the client to see the light. Persuasion involves managing the expectations of the client, in effect keeping them well below what a lawyer may or may not be able to prove.

When a lawyer appears before a judge he must effectively persuade this finder of law. Although courtroom decorum and respect are important, concise argument of facts and law are even more so. Every judge appreciates an attorney who gets right to the crux of the matter without preliminaries and side shows. The court's time is valuable and a direct approach regarding facts and arguments, pros as well as cons of one's case, will garner great appreciation from the bench. The veteran lawyer is very careful to avoid disparaging his opposing counsel. There is no quicker way to alienate a judge than to attack a colleague. A smart attorney will effectively and honestly question the legal arguments and only the legal arguments of opposing counsel. Collegiality is crucial to the effective presentation of any legal argument to the court. The objective here is to disagree without being disagreeable. The goal is to keep the "civil" in civil litigation. By being likable, the veteran lawyer may even persuade his worthy opponent of his viewpoint.

The final persuasive efforts are directed at the jury itself. Attorneys must shape and comment on the facts of the case. The lawyer's comments, however, are not evidence. Evidence must be presented in a light most favorable to the client. This is not deception. It is rather fact shaping. One particular method for persuading a jury is a twist on the old kindergarten adage: "show and tell." Well-known trial lawyer David Ball states the issue succinctly: "Show, not tell, the jury" about your case. This requires humility and proving your case in a humble manner. It shows the jury why you should win without authoritatively telling them what to do. This is called the soft sell. It is a respectful sell to a jury. Low key persuasion is the quickest path to success. For example, the "show not tell" approach can be applied to sales of a product or service. The idea is not only to show why your product or service is superior, but to convince your prospect that it is in their own self-interest to purchase your product or service. Such an approach makes them feel that they are part of the process.

For instance, in a motor vehicle crash case a jury may be persuaded that public safety is the highest interest at trial. By finding against an unsafe driving defendant, safety is preserved. In essence, the lawyer is appealing to a higher purpose that we can all agree on. Self-interest is not a dirty phrase, but rather comports with the notion that charity begins at home. Obviously, selfishness is not appropriate, but self-interest is. We appeal to one's self interest via this skill. With such an approach, we not only persuade, but we satisfy the notion: "everybody wins." The jury feels that they have won by awarding a verdict, which is not only in the plaintiff's best interest, but in their own as well. See *David Ball on Damages: A Plaintiff Attorney's Guide to Damages* (David Ball 2011).

Direct and cross examination utilize questions to filter out and distill relevant evidence in any trial. A jury trial is limited in time and scope. Therefore it is critical for the lawyer to get to the point. Questions allow the attorney to arrive at said point in an efficient manner. In a sense, the lawyer distills the important facts of the case to soundbites of true substance. These soundbites are typically the question and the answer. They are very brief and to the point, but also memorable. The "$64,000 question", the pause, and finally the answer are indelibly imprinted on the jury's collective mind.

We use the question/answer formula because of the innate, limited attention span of the human mind. Again, this may seem like a shortcut, but it is a clever shortcut that is priceless to the veteran lawyer's tool box. Socrates would have been proud of the evolution of his simple philosophy of arriving at the truth via direct examination and cross examination. Direct exam affords the witness a semi-narrative, descriptive response to a very open ended question.

A brief review of cross examination basics is in order. Cross examination, unlike direct examination, limits the witness to yes/no answers. Direct examination is the long form; cross examination is the short form. The cross examination sequence prohibits a witness from giving an open ended response. Typically the witness is adverse to the cross examiner. Lawyers do not want to give a narrative question to an adverse witness for fear that damaging, unpredictable, information will be disclosed. This is known as information containment. Lawyers are very careful to shape the facts of a case to convey only the contained facts he wishes the jury to see. His opponent will do the same. Through this vetting process, the jury will ultimately hear all of the facts, good and bad.

The cross examination process presumes that the lawyer already knows the answer to the question and is simply ratifying that knowledge via leading questions. It is intended to poke holes through the legal positions of the opponent's case. It can be very effective if the lawyer can portray the illusion that the adverse witness agrees with him. Cross examination is typically limited to a very few questions. It is an in-and-out military operation. The objective is to do as much damage as possible and then get out quickly.

Typically a witness will never completely agree with the opposing lawyer on cross examination. The witness may, however, agree on two to three critical points. Once these points are made, the objective is to not linger on the cross examination stage. By extracting a handful of valuable concessions from an adverse witness, their testimony can be effectively neutralized. There is one word of warning about cross examination: It should rarely be practiced outside of a court room. From a practical standpoint, the cross exam is sure to generate hard feelings. No one likes to be cornered by an interrogator. A gentler approach to questioning can still make the point effectively.

A final point regarding the questioning process must be considered. The point is that all questions need not be answered. Sometimes no response is the best course of inaction. In the courtroom, a deposition, or classroom, there is no choice. But outside of these venues, this maxim applies: An open book is a great thing. But do not be one yourself. By not answering purposeless, curiosity-satisfying questions, you develop leverage and a bit of mystery about yourself. You place yourself above the interrogator. The lesson here is to avoid submitting yourself to the whims of some self-appointed questioner. Remember, questions in and of themselves are not evidence. Don't let anyone tell you that he who is silent, assents.

f. On Your Feet Thinking Skills

Quick-thinking skills are primarily employed by a lawyer during normal court appearances such as appellate arguments, district court motions, jury trials, as well as depositions. A lawyer must be quick without being careless. She must respond speedily to objections, which could eliminate portions of her case. She thereafter must find an alternate method to get her evidence before the court. Conversely, the attorney has to make an immediate objection on the record or said objection is waived forever.

The quick-thinking lawyer is always fully cognizant of the cardinal rule: expect the unexpected. Because we are dealing with human beings, nothing will go according to script. Questions, answers, and issues will arise, which are totally off script. They may be unexpected and often hostile. The best defense against these situations is complete and total preparation.

It requires one to be conversant with the facts of one's case. Once the lawyer has absorbed the details and facts of the case, including specifics about their own client as well as specifics about witnesses, it becomes a part of them. This is the essence of preparation. Law professors, judges, and opposing counsel are notorious for attempting to upset an attorney's presentation by raising non-issues This is deliberate. In many situations these individuals attempt to get you to "swing at a pitch in the dirt." It is the attorney's job to weave in his argument repeatedly in every answer before the court.

The thorough and complete knowledge of your case facts will provide you with a "zone" of quick reaction and quick-thinking in any situation. This immersion produces a flow of fast responses, which is second nature. The zone has been described by professional athletes as a mental and physical flow of clear-headed productive thought and action. This is similar to a quarterback in the NFL who marches his team down the field with one pass after another, one perfect play after another that finally reaches the end zone. Professional athletes love the zone. They are actually performing without even thinking. They are performing on instinct, which is a direct result of full preparation over the previous week. In order to access the "zone" in the business world, complete and thorough knowledge of one's product and service is mandatory. Examples of this range from your presentation with barely a notecard to the sheer ease and flow of correctly answering all questions thrown at you.

Furthermore, the illusion of quick thinking can be provided by canned phrases that a lawyer already has in his arsenal. Those soundbites, if you will, can be drawn upon in any situation. Again, this is preparation, not necessarily quick thinking, but it provides the illusion. Quick-thinking is not as quick as we think it is. The rapid response from a lawyer is simply part of the flow and provides the added illusion that the lawyer is smarter than he really is. He's not simply smart. He's simply prepared. The lesson here is clear: be humble enough to prepare.

A final point here is that thinking on one's feet is truly literal. The mere act of moving around allows us to think better. Standing immovable at a podium for too long can inhibit the thinking process. You can get literally stuck or mentally frozen by remaining in one position. Walking and moving about can melt that big brain freeze. So move around at any opportunity.

g. People Skills

A lawyer's people skills are, to modify an Abraham Lincoln quote, truly "an attorney's stock in trade." Without people skills, a lawyer will have no business. Without people skills, a lawyer cannot empathize or relate to his client or persuade a jury. These skills require an attorney to be pleasant and civil with all individuals he comes into contact with. They allow a lawyer to read his opponent, the judge, and his own client. It's not just about the lawyer's case and his client's interests. He must be acutely aware of the needs of the judge, jury and even the needs of opposing counsel as well.

People skills allow a lawyer to become cooperative during the legal process. The practice of law is not simply one battle after another. The practice of law in 90 percent of cases requires cooperation and compromise. Each side does not get everything it wants and frankly never will. Typically this translates into resolution of a case via a monetary out of court settlement. If it is a criminal case, it is resolved through a plea bargain.

The general idea here is that lawyers, via their people skills, must see the other side's case as clearly as their own. They realize that their client's case will be analyzed by a twelve member jury who will be more than happy to look at both sides, not just one. It is this ability to see both sides of the coin, which is the greatest lawyer skill of all.

Imagine if you will, a Kennedy half dollar. On one side we have JFK in profile. On the other we have the presidential coat of arms. Now suppose we rubbed out just one side of the coin so that it is perfectly smooth. We now would have a one-sided coin. Of what value is a one sided coin? It literally tells only half the story. This metaphor instructs us to understand the other guy's side too. This is how we become just. This is known as "legal empathy." There is no greater diversity than actually placing oneself in the mental shoes of the other guy. Legal empathy is essential to success in and out of the courtroom. The ability to empathize is the single most important formula for such success.

The adversarial nature of lawyering demands continuous communication with an opposing lawyer. Although the preferred course is collegiality with our counterparts, sometimes their behavior makes this next to impossible. The best remedy is the written email or letter. It is probably best not to engage an unreasonable lawyer via impersonal meetings or phone contact. When dealing with an unreasonable opponent, the written communication sends a very formal message. Furthermore, it protects the lawyer by creating a well-documented file.

Your adversary must eventually respond in writing to your written communication. A pattern of written correspondence will eventually ensue, giving a full history of the communication with dates and times between the two attorneys. This is similar to the partner memo, but continuous over a longer period of time. This ice cold correspondence should eliminate any emotion of the moment and maintain a business tone at all times. If there is emotion when initially typing or dictating this written correspondence, it is best not to send it immediately. It is best to come back to it later in the day when your emotion has subsided and you can dispassionately revise and make corrections to said letter or even refuse to send it at all. A cooling off period is priceless in this regard.

Lawyers tend to maintain a very serious, humorless tone when it comes to business. Once again, civility is the priority, but an attorney must maintain his "poker face" in order to conceal his true feelings or intentions. This is known as "cold skill civility." Furthermore, the poker face should act as a guard against displaying one's reaction to any information received.

For instance, most people rely upon facial expressions, voice tone, and overall body language to interpret what is occurring. Cold skill civility takes the body language component out of the equation. If the attorney continuously demonstrates a granite facial expression during a deposition or a motion, he becomes very difficult to read. The lawyer then becomes a bit of a mystery and this magnifies his presence tenfold. Unreadability is a very valuable commodity in the lawyer's toolbox. Being impossible to read can throw your opponent off and deprive them of something to lock onto. It is particularly valuable in the business setting, meeting, or negotiation.

An attorney must be sensitive to their client's interests and to understand where they are coming from. A lawyer must understand that his client may be under great financial and psychological pressure with patience running in short supply. All of the personal and monetary interests of the participants in any case must be juggled by the "people skilled" attorney. Above all else, the attorney must not only stand up for his client, but stand up to them as well. The simple fact is that lawyer and client may disagree deeply on case evaluation and strategy. The skilled attorney endeavors to not just advise a client what they can do under the law, but what they ought to do as well.

He must be very careful however not to substitute his own judgement for that of the client.

People skills are also about listening to the client or the witness, the defense lawyer, or the judge. We must give them full attention and be there 100 percent. A lawyer cannot be thinking about his next question while questioning a witness. A lawyer does not ask questions in a robotic scripted manner, but rather is fluid, and flexible in changing the course of questioning based upon the answers. The same applies to responding to court questions during a motion or oral argument. Sometimes the court is even trying to help the attorney with an easy soft ball question that, if the attorney is actually listening, he can hit right out of the stadium.

Likability is a final people skill. Frankly, most people expect lawyers to be complete and total arrogant jerks. Society has that expectation. The smart lawyer has the unique ability to "out-nice" everybody in the room. They should have the ability to be pleasant, not condescending. They can explain clearly complex topics without being arrogant. It is a very heady thing to go through years of law school, a bar exam, and finally to acquire a law license. The veteran lawyer will not allow this to go to his head. He will seek to serve his customer no matter how successful he is. No matter how many million dollar verdicts he has obtained, he will display a conversant, simple manner that all can understand. This requires a great deal of patience and civility. But in the end, these will translate into the most important characteristic of all: likability. If a jury likes the attorney and doesn't like the client, he can still win. If a judge likes the attorney but not the facts, a likable lawyer can still win.

h. Research Skills

Research skills are also valuable weapons in the legal arsenal. Lawyers conduct a systematic, orderly search pattern when they attack a legal problem. There will be many legal issues that come up that were never taught in law school. These unexplored issues require thorough research in a law library. This research is much easier with the advent of the Internet. Now one can access a data base of words that lead to the proper topic and ultimately to the proper answer. Synonyms allow us to access more information, and those words will even lead to more words to reach a resolution.

For instance, an attorney may have to research general principles of negligence if he is representing a client in a medical malpractice claim. Negligence may be a helpful term, but other terms such as doctor/patient, ethics violations, medical malpractice, insurance coverage, duty, and breach of duty, may all be related terms that lead one to the correct answer or controlling case. The trick to any legal research is to find key phrases and key words that lead to similar concepts. This process allows the lawyer to expand his horizons, which can uncover that one crucial case or statute that controls his set of facts and ultimately wins the case.

In many respects this legal research is painstaking and requires accessing a number of legal sources. This can involve articles on the topic in addition to cases and statutes. The point here is that the lawyer must exhaust all avenues to make sure the topic is thoroughly covered. There may even be entire books on the topic in question. Furthermore, attorneys take advantage of works authored by other lawyers. These consist of manuals that lawyers write for other lawyers. These are known as continuing legal education publications. These manuals are provided to lawyers who attend seminars in order to maintain legal education credits and therefore their license. The value here is that such manuals are written by lawyers specifically for lawyers. Thought of another way, these are essentially trade journals. As we can see, a lawyer's legal education does not stop at his law school graduation ceremony.

The greatest gift that legal research gives us is self-reliance. Lawyers, as a group, are notorious for refusing the help of others in favor of their own research skills. Attorneys are taught from day one the following maxim: "Look up the damn issue yourself." They do not ask for advice as a first option, but rather as a last resort. Herein lies the greatest value of such research skills: in life and business it is so important to try and solve one's problems first on one's own.

The aloneness, the solitude of researching a great problem is a confidence builder. Slogging through this process builds the core of self-reliance. Without the effort of such attempts, you are forever relying upon the charity of others to solve your problems. This results in unnecessary dependence upon others. Only after exhaustive research and effort should one ask for the advice of others. The Internet alone eliminates all excuses for not making these research attempts on your own.

The second best research tool that lawyers and non-lawyers can use is a seminar or conversation with someone who has done it before. A wealth of information can be mined from a person who has handled a similar case before, versus reinventing the wheel. Conversing with someone who has "been there, done that" is incredibly efficient. This simple method can save you weeks, if not years, of research and effort. The hidden value of such conversation is that you are hearing from a person conveying battlefield experiences. It is practical information, not always the theoretical, that counts.

Unfortunately, books and manuals can be all too theoretical. It is the "real time" application of these rules and procedures that truly makes it practical for the rest of us to apply in our lives. Theory is essentially "a read book" remaining on the shelf with no practical application. Street smarts is the actual use of that book. One cannot stand upon a single resource that gives you comfort. The conclusion here is that one must access a diversity of resources.

i. Problem-Solving Skills

Lawyers in many ways are like mathematicians. They aggressively attack a problem with a formula. Their approach is anything but casual. They are given a problem and told to solve it. People come to lawyers with their problems. Usually these are big problems that present a significant crisis in the client's life. Most lawyers are proud to be at the side of their client to shepherd them through a very difficult time in their life. The lawyer, in essence, provides problem-solving services. He will gather the necessary information (facts) and then apply the law. Good lawyers read the law over and over again to be absolutely sure they are applying it correctly. Nuances and new interpretations reveal themselves through this process. The lawyer then can advise his client of the application of the law to the client's own unique fact situation. Thereafter, a course of action can be designed.

Furthermore, the lawyer will game out various scenarios that can occur down the line. He will give his client a list of pros and cons on settlement offers versus taking the matter to trial. Most importantly, in the problem-solving aspect, the lawyer will advise his clients of his or her rights and obligations under the law. Obviously, everyone has rights, which tend to be of paramount concern. For instance, they may feel their rights are violated by some particular defendant. But the client must also be apprised of his obligations under the law to take proper steps and to take them in the proper order to preserve those very rights. The lawyer continuously holds this two-edged sword in mind as he represents his client. In the final analysis, the client must decide on their own. The attorney can do everything but decide for the client.

I cannot emphasize the importance of "gaming out" scenarios. This is simply looking into the future and analyzing the combinations and permutations of a chosen course of action. To some degree it allows us to predict into the future what the possible consequences are of a certain action. It's looking down the road at what can happen if we set into motion a certain action. If we present a certain argument to our jury it's important to predict or game out a typical reaction that a jury may have to this argument. It's looking down the line at the results of the fire storm you create through your own actions. If you light that match, what fire storm can occur? Who would be affected? Who would be burned? How far and how long will the fire storm continue? Also, not only actions must be gamed out, but inaction as well. If we chose to leave a certain thing alone, what will the result be? How will the inaction be perceived? Remember, perception in many cases is reality.

The practicing lawyer is able to analyze a fact situation to death in order to properly apply the law to said facts. There are many nuances in facts that can win a case or lose a case. In most situations, the lawyer will shape those facts to achieve a desired result. Problem solving requires that a lawyer not only know the facts of his client's case but that of his opponent as well. Once again, like a coin, he must be able to see both sides in order to achieve a well-rounded understanding of the case as a whole.

There are going to be weaknesses and strengths on each side of the ledger. Some facts may provide the lawyer with leverage. If there is a criminal conviction or criminal record in the defendant's background, he can use that as leverage. Some facts may be excluded by the rules of evidence before a jury. But they can still have value to be used as leverage. Leverage, in essence, is pressure. In most cases it is a threat. But the lawyer can legally utilize that leverage. This leverage is also part of negotiation skills. For instance, the threat of a lawsuit or the threat of a deposition constitutes legal leverage applied to extract a settlement from the other side. In any other arena outside of law this would be extortion or blackmail. This particular type of leverage makes unpleasant facts abundantly clear to the opponent.

j. Absorption and Retention Skills

Attorneys consistently absorb and retain data and input. This data can be in the form of documentation. It can be in the form of court decisions. Input can also be a client's or hostile witness's body language. By absorbing as well as listening, the lawyer becomes one with the witness. By doing so he can more effectively ferret out inconsistencies which impact the credibility of the witness as a whole.

At the beginning of a case the most important part of absorption comes at the initial interview with the client. The lawyer must size up and absorb the initial presentation of their story. The veteran lawyer in many situations is a very careful and focused listener. He gives the gift of attention to his client at the initial meeting and during the early minutes of the interview may not even take notes. Sometimes taking notes can detract from attentiveness. The idea is that the lawyer listens acutely to the client's problems as well as goals. There may be overt goals or there may be a hidden client agenda. The lawyer then can help the client achieve these goals within the bounds of ethics and law.

A lawyer uses repetition in order to effectively absorb critical information. The old adage: "repetition is the mother of skill" is particularly applicable to trial lawyers. Records, the law, cases, court orders must be read more than once to effectively imprint said information. By the time of trial, the critical information is so ingrained in the lawyer's mind that he can recall it as a matter of second nature. Being conversant with the facts of one's case in life is critical to presenting your side of any issue. Having facts at your fingertips via the absorption/retentive process is invaluable. Rote memory is still a critical tool regarding retention of basic legal concepts. Why? Because rote memorization forces one to know the elements of basic theories. You should be a walking bundle of rote memories.

The veteran lawyer knows his product inside and out. He sells it with great people skills. Mature lawyers are all about prepared effort. Casual presentation or "winging it" is the enemy of preparation.

Preparation is essentially learning far in advance, and not during the presentation itself. We must learn ahead of time. We should not be learning as the gavel falls in the courtroom of life.

k. Advocacy Skills and the 4C's

Every great lawyer or nonlawyer must have the ability to advocate for another human being without judgement. Lawyers achieve this by employing the 4C's of advocacy. They are comfort, constancy, counsel, and confidentiality. The DUI (Driving under the influence) scenario is a classic legal example, aptly illustrating the 4C's.

When the attorney initially meets with the accused client, it is typically in a jail setting. The attorney and the client are separated by a thick glass partition. They may not even be allowed to shake hands at their initial meeting. The lawyer will deliver an immediate sense of comfort to the unfortunate client. This is a quantum of solace or measure of comfort as it were. The client will be reassured and informed that this is not the end of the world. For the first time in several hours, the accused realizes that he has an ally who will render assistance at this difficult time. The client now realizes that he does not walk alone as he confronts the criminal justice system. This great relief and comfort steels the accused for the remaining time in jail and the difficult days ahead.

In addition to comfort, there is the notion of constancy. The attorney provides a constant presence to the client. This presence occurs at not only the initial meeting, but at every court appearance, including trial. During this time the lawyer assists the client in navigating a complex legal system. The lawyer provides this presence without fail. In addition, the attorney advocates solely for the client's interests and no one else's. Constancy tells us that the accused will not be abandoned and that his advocate will never leave his side.

The third element of advocacy is counsel. This simply refers to sound and practical advice. Counsel involves explaining the law substantively and procedurally. Substance refers to the hows and whys as well as the technicalities of law itself. Procedure refers to courtroom "rules of the game" that we all must all play by. Counsel finally demands that the attorney explain the risks of trial as opposed to an "out of court" plea bargain. Now that the counseling element is complete, the client can make an informed and correct decision as to their case.

The fourth and final element is confidentiality. All discussions between lawyer and client are strictly confidential. This applies to tactics, strategies, advice as well as private information divulged by the client. This means that the attorney is the keeper of client secrets and can never be compelled to breach such a trust.

The combination of these 4C's of advocacy ensures the proper protection of a client's interests. These four elements can truly be applied by any one of us in our dealings with others. They require us to honor the dignity of those we seek to help. Advocacy is essentially speaking up for those who cannot speak for themselves. This checklist helps us advocate for other human beings who cannot advocate for themselves. If you seek to help someone in trouble, follow the 4C's to the letter.

BLACK LETTER LAW

- Be up front regarding the pros and cons of your goods or services. Your customer will respect you for it.
- Negotiation is a forum wherein the parties trade something of value between each other. Beware the "phantom offer."
- Immediate doing demands the performance of tasks while they are still fresh in one's mind.
- Deadlines are good. They compel us to do what we otherwise would not do for ourselves.
- Do not tolerate the unfinished job with your name on it.
- Lawyers recognize the duty to read. "The large print giveth. The fine print taketh away." -Fulton Sheen
- Be precise in your own diction and maintain a granite disposition in all business matters.
- When it comes to your presentation: "Show, not tell." -David Ball
- If a one-sided coin is valueless, a one-sided argument is just as unacceptable.
- Don't be arrogant, but "out-nice" the other guy.
- Always research the issues on your own first.
- Employ the four C's of advocacy: Comfort, Counsel, Constancy, and Confidentiality.
- Legal empathy is essential to success.
- Winging it is the enemy of preparation.

CHAPTER 5

Ethical Attorney Thinking

This final chapter is directed at what lawyers should not do. This is negative reinforcement if you will. Lawyers unfortunately have been stereotyped as dishonest, amoral barracudas who will stop at nothing to achieve a victory for their client. It has been said that lawyers do not cross the line. They simply start on the other side of it. Unfortunately, this is a common misconception. What is not so common is the fact that lawyers are heavily regulated by various court rules. Some of these rules are aspirational but most are mandatory.

These particular rules fall into the three categories of professional aspirations, rules of professional conduct, as well as a code of judicial conduct for judges. They serve as an honor code of conduct for all attorneys and judges. The benefit here is that various portions of these rules can be utilized by you in your attempt to become more ethical in your own career. It would behoove all of us to become intimately familiar with the ethical rules of our company, employer and profession. Be sure to access your governing handbook and actually read it. At this point, I would like to mention that all attorneys owe an ethical duty to represent their clients competently. I try to avoid the term "zealously." That term hints at emotional involvement by the lawyer. Let's just say that a lawyer must maximize his representation of the client within the bounds of the law. Also, please note that the attorney owes such a duty to the one client. I repeat, the singular client. There is no duty to the public at large or public policy. The lawyer cannot ,and should not, represent the world.

Professional Aspirations

Professional aspirations are exactly that. They are a set of professional desires aimed at the best of lawyerly conduct. They are not mandatory, but rather seek to encourage attorneys to comport themselves according to the highest standards in law practice as well as courtroom appearances. The *Minnesota Rules of Court /MN Professional Aspirations* (2018) Eagan, Minnesota: Thomson West address several professional aspirations. Here a few examples:

> A lawyer owes personal dignity, integrity, and independence to the administration of justice. A lawyer's conduct should be characterized at all times by a personal courtesy and professional integrity in the fullest sense of those terms. (MPA I)

These aspirations further direct that lawyers must conduct their affairs with candor and honesty. Furthermore, their word must be their bond. Aspirations in essence require a lawyer to go above and beyond the call when it comes to honesty with the court and opposing counsel. An attorney has a duty to represent his client, but he must do so within the bounds of honesty and the law. Attorneys must demonstrate proper conduct at all times. This means not only core propriety but the strict avoidance of the appearance of impropriety.

Courtroom formality truly inspires a maximum business tone to be employed by all participants. This anti-casual approach gets the job done with great efficiency. There is simply no tolerance for a relaxed demeanor in the courtroom. This philosophy is transferable to all business transactions and meetings. Consistent exercise of protocol and formality will make you the most reasonable and respected person in the room.

Respect for the ultimate authority, the judge, is a given. Many times the judge will be incorrect on rulings or just plain nasty to counsel. Even if the lawyer is correct on a point, speaking truth to power is seldom in the interests of the client. Remember, the judge is not always right, but he is always the judge. The attorney must be the ultimate diplomat when it comes to the powers that be. This means they must deftly make their point in an unemotional way. Their position should be made in a respectful manner in a consummate business tone. An "all business" demeanor is the best defense against a difficult judge or any opponent. The business tone is anti-business casual. It clearly forces your opponent to adopt a more respectful tone to you in return. This no nonsense approach will always pay great dividends in return.

As far as the relationship between the attorney and the client, lawyers owe all of their skills and loyalty to said client in the effort to protect and advance their legitimate rights and interests. An additional important point is that the aspirational rules make it clear that clients cannot demand that a lawyer engage in abusive or offensive conduct in the prosecution of their case. Furthermore, no unethical conduct may be committed nor encouraged. A final point regarding lawyers and clients is that the litigation must be done expeditiously and as economically as possible. Undue delay is unethical.

These aspirational rules regarding clients also apply to conduct between lawyers:

> A lawyer owes courtesy, candor, cooperation, and compliance with all agreements and mutual understandings to opposing counsel in the conduct of an office practice and in pursuit of the resolution of legal issues... Conduct that may be characterized as uncivil, abrasive, abusive, hostile, or obstructive impedes the fundamental goal of resolving disputes rationally, peacefully, and efficiently. (MPA III)

This rule keeps the "civil" in civil litigation. It requires simply that there be no sand bagging of your opponent. It discourages personal attacks and dishonesty as well. Courtesy and punctuality for all court appearances is required. Prompt and civil responses to written communications are also encouraged. This rule also emphasizes that we must be rational in order to resolve disputes efficiently. The rule discourages undue emotion, which will certainly cloud our own judgement.

Another important aspirational rule between attorneys states as follows:

> We will disagree without being disagreeable. We recognize that effective representation does not require antagonistic or obnoxious behavior. (MPA III4)

The preceding aspirational rule essentially says that we can in all business situations agree to disagree without getting personal or hostile in the process. This dovetails with the general application of unemotional skills in the business world. This "poker face" approach is important as it conceals your true feelings when it comes to business transactions. Impassivity and courtesy can and must coexist.

A third component of aspirational rules deals with the lawyer/judge relationship. It essentially says that each owes a duty of respect to the other. It is important to realize that lawyers and judges are responsible to protect the dignity and independence of the court and the profession. Both should seek to avoid unjust and improper criticism and attack. Diligence, respect, and punctuality are the pillars of conduct between lawyers and judges. The duty to speak and write civilly is also required as well as preparedness for all court appearances and conferences. This rule in particular focuses on the duty to prepare, to be ready to present arguments in an economical and timely fashion. As we learned in Chapter 1, the worst admission that a law student can make to a professor is "I am unprepared." Such a statement to a judge would be nothing short of catastrophic in the courtroom.

Furthermore, attorneys owe a duty to the court to never bring disorder or disruption to the courtroom and must also advise our clients and witnesses accordingly. A word on punctuality deserves mention. "On time" attendance for any important function should be strictly self-enforced. Simply arriving at the scheduled event fifteen minutes early is the best defense against tardiness. To do otherwise disrespects others and destroys your credibility in the process.

Another aspiration, as far as the attorney's conduct in the courtroom, states the following:

> If we observe a lawyer being uncivil to others, we will call it to the attention of the offending lawyer on our own initiative. (MPA IVB2)

This particular aspiration is essentially calling another lawyer out on their conduct with immediacy. This a far cry from inaction. It requires a lawyer to get actively involved and do the right thing when he sees an injustice or misconduct occurring. The lawyer cannot sit idly by. Their profession demands proactive involvement.

The last point regarding professional aspirations requires in one sentence a very important type of conduct, which we all can aspire to:

> We will give the issues in controversy deliberate, impartial, and studious analysis and consideration. (MPA IV7)

This is a required duty of judges and lawyers alike. This method is the foundation for thinking like an attorney. We can all apply this type of careful analysis in our daily problems. It means being prepared for any professional appointment or event on our calendar. It requires dispassionate analysis without getting personal about it. It is essentially a requirement that we delete emotion in favor of impartial studied analysis and consideration. This demands complete consideration of any issues at hand in a business-like fashion. In order to achieve this, we must first avoid getting upset and keep our heads.

In sum, the aspirational rules can be used by all of us to effectively achieve our goals. These goals are professional courtesy, civility, and preparedness. We can go much further in life if we employ them on a consistent basis. Courtrooms and judges will not allow inconsistent behavior in this regard. It is not a "sometimes" proposition. It is a deal-breaker in the courtroom and should be a deal-breaker in the courtroom of our lives as well.

Rules of Professional Conduct

The legal field requires strict adherence to rules of professional conduct. As examples I will again cite from the *Minnesota Rules of Court/ Rules of Professional Conduct.* These rules are different from professional aspirations as they are *mandatory*. Adherence to these rules is nonnegotiable. If a lawyer does run afoul of these rules, he can be punished by public/private admonition, suspension, or disbarment. This strict code of conduct must be followed by all lawyers. Also, if another lawyer sees a violation of this conduct by a colleague, they have a duty to report it. This is known as the "rat on your friends doctrine."

To begin with, a lawyer must provide competent representation to a client. This requires "legal knowledge, skill, thoroughness, and preparation reasonably necessary for the representation."(MRPC 1.1) The attorney has a further duty to maintain competence by completing continuing legal education seminars as well as continuous examination of court decisions issued every week. It requires a lawyer to essentially maintain a record of knowledge and skill by keeping abreast of changes in the law. As the law is continually changing and fluid, a lawyer must stay on top of their area of specialty.

"A lawyer must also be diligent and prompt in representing his clients".(MRPC 1.3) In addition, "lawyers may not knowingly reveal information relating to the representation of a client".(MRPC 1.6)

Of course, if the client consents to the revelation, this rule would not apply. Essentially, an attorney must protect the secrets of a client. This is known as client/attorney privilege. This is very similar to the priest /penitent or doctor/patient confidentiality. However, the lawyer can disclose if it is reasonably calculated to prevent fraud or the commission of a crime.

Lawyers must also be careful to avoid conflicts of interest. In other words, a lawyer cannot represent a client if the representation involves a current conflict of interest. This involves representation of two or more clients, which materially limits the lawyer's responsibilities to another client. Some disclosure is allowed, perhaps to continue representation as long as both parties are aware and consent. In essence, this rule indicates that a lawyer cannot serve two masters, and essentially, he must make a choice. Finally, a lawyer cannot use information obtained through one client to the detriment of the other. Insider trading by lawyers is not allowed.

Lawyers are also required to maintain the integrity of their own profession.

> "Lawyers cannot knowingly make a false statement of material fact or fail to disclose a fact necessary to correct misapprehension known by the person to have arisen in the matter…" (MRPC 4.1)

Furthermore, if a lawyer knows that another lawyer has committed a violation of the Rules of Professional Conduct that raises a substantial question as to that lawyer's honesty, trustworthiness, or fitness as a lawyer in other respects, he shall inform the appropriate professional authority. (MRPC 8.3).

Finally, there is a list of actions entitled "misconduct" under MRPC 8.4. This prohibits criminal acts that reflect adversely on the lawyer's integrity. It further covers conduct involving dishonesty, fraud, deceit, or misrepresentation and further, any conduct prejudicial to the administration of justice. It also precludes harassment on the basis of race, age, creed, religion, colors, national origin, disability, sexual orientation, or marital status in connection with the lawyer's professional activities.

Essentially, these Rules of Professional Conduct provide a sampling of a basic honor code, which is expected of all lawyers in their professional activities as well as their outside private activities. It requires a higher standard of conduct than the general population. If we seek to conduct ourselves in compliance with these rules in our own lives, we too can achieve the highest level of integrity, honesty, and class that may not have been otherwise possible.

These particular rules require a high degree of honesty and candor in all dealings. Many similar rules can be found in company policies. As a lawyer is familiar with these rules of the game, you should be familiar as well with the rules of your own employer. Both sets of rules are applicable for not only our professional lives, but our private lives as well. They are guideposts to keep us on the straight and narrow. These rules are not easy rules. They require the highest continuous level of conduct. More succinctly, correct conduct is the standard. As lawyers are professionals, they are required to comport with the highest of standards. But you don't have to be a lawyer to comply. You simply have to know your own ethical rules.

The general advice here is to take the best of these standards and apply them effectively in your own lives. It's a code of honor that you can actually use. These ethical basics are not just for lawyers. The public relations problem that attorneys face arises from the fact that the legal system is an adversarial one. In its wake the system leaves a winner and a loser. Only an out-of-court settlement can eradicate the win-lose scenario allowing both sides to save face. The essential thrust is that these particular rules of conduct and aspirations guide the attorney in self-regulating their own behavior. Lawyers are not the only ones regulated by rules. As we shall see, judicial appointees are also heavily regulated.

Judicial Rules of Conduct

The third and final conduct code applies to judges and is known as the Code of Judicial Conduct. The Code of Judicial Conduct is also contained in the *Minnesota Rules of Court*. Firstly, this is a code of judicial conduct, not a code of "Judge Judy" conduct. Ideally, judges should represent the absolute best in courtroom behavior. In many ways the judge is a patient father or mother presiding over the oftentimes unruly lawyers, jurors, and staff of their household. The first relevant judicial canon states as follows:

> A judge shall act at all times in a manner that promotes public confidence in the independence, integrity, and impartiality of the judiciary, and shall avoid impropriety and the appearance of impropriety. Furthermore the judge shall avoid abuse of the prestige of his judicial office. Essentially, this means a judge cannot advance his own personal or economic interests of himself or others. (MCJC 1.3)

Furthermore, a judge must uphold and apply the law and shall perform all duties fairly and impartially. (MCJC 2.2) This means a judge cannot be swayed by public clamor or fear of criticism. A judge cannot be influenced by social, family, political, financial, or other interests or relationships when it comes to his judicial conduct or judgement. (MCJC 2.4) Judges are required to be competent, diligent, and cooperative, and must also ensure that everyone has a right to be heard. Settlement of differences is encouraged but cannot be coerced. In addition, judges require order and decorum in their courtrooms. "A judge shall be patient, dignified, and courteous to litigants, jurors, witnesses, lawyers, court staff, and court officials, and others with whom the judge deals in an official capacity..." (MCJC 2.8)

Once again, politeness, patience, and dignity count in the courtroom setting. Even the judge herself is not exempt. The actual rules of high conduct are quite contrary to many of the judges who are portrayed on television and in cinema. In real life, judges and attorneys are low key and civil. The two most important things a judge can lend to the process are eminent fairness and the sense of being heard. The first, fairness, requires that every litigant in the end believes that they received a "fair shake" from the judge. Win or lose, they must feel that they were treated justly by the court. The second, and no less important, is that the litigants believe that they were heard by the court. This concept requires active and meaningful listening and the appearance thereof. Meaningful fairness and listening are the cornerstones of success in all business and personal relationships. If one can master these concepts in business dealings success is assured.

Let's not forget that everyone tends to be on their best behavior in front of a judge. The judicial bench is three times higher than an ordinary counsel table for a reason. It promotes a visual sense of order, authority, and decorum. This compels anyone in the courtroom to aspire to impeccable behavior. One can never go wrong by employing good, solid courtroom behavior. You simply cannot lose if you are the most serious and formal person in the room.

This particular chapter will now conclude with an important point. These rules, although positive in their affirmations, tend to focus on negative behavior. It is the do's and don'ts of being a lawyer that are contained in these rules. We have all heard of Dr. Norman Vincent Peale's book, *The Power of Positive Thinking*. As we examine the rules of conduct, there are a great many don'ts. These represent "the power of negative thinking". Sometimes negative rules can be more effective in controlling our behavior than positive ones. Consider the "thou shalt nots" in the Ten Commandments. The aforementioned ethical laws provide standards and measurements for human behavior. It places necessary limits on human behavior for the greater good.

BLACK LETTER LAW

- Professional aspirations aim at the best of lawyerly conduct.
- Ethical rules are essentially negative reinforcements to behavior.
- Dignity, professional integrity, candor, and honesty are the touchstones of the ethical attorney.
- The judge is not always right, but he is always the judge.
- We must disagree without being disagreeable.
- Diligence, respect and punctuality are the pillars of conduct between lawyers and judges.
- A lawyer must be diligent, prompt, and competent in the representation of a client.
- Attorneys owe confidentiality to their client. They are the keepers of client secrets.
- Be familiar with the ethical rules and values of your company.
- The judge owes politeness, patience, and dignity to the participants in their courtroom.
- Ethical rules place necessary limits on human behavior for the greater good.
- Endeavor to employ solid courtroom behavior in the business world.

Conclusion

I hope that the purpose of this book has been clear: legal thinking is "power thinking." Lawyerly thought employs a formality of mental discipline. It is not easy to discipline our own patterns of thought. It is hard to discard casual, soft habits of thinking. Law-based thought forces us to maintain a fusion between rigorous, ordered thought and behavior. The good news is that such ordered thought places us head and shoulders above casual thought. If we distill it down, legal thought is nothing more than "power logic" employed to govern our behavior in the business world. The law has always employed exceptional thinking that is transferable, sturdy, and useful. Law is for everyone and by extension anyone can think like an attorney.

The design of the chapters was quite deliberate. My overall intent was to show the evolution of thought from law school all the way to veteran lawyer sprinkled with ethical rules of conduct. This evolution shows that over time we mature and get better in our own thinking ability. The overall tenor of this book addresses unemotional rational thought coupled with impeccable behavior and preparation. This can lead us to not only understand the other guy's point of view, but if necessary, argue that view as well. This is the essence of diversity, plain and simple. Such powerful thinking enables a more complete and well-rounded understanding of the problem at hand. With better thinking comes stronger problem solving. The added bonus is that the mere knowledge of law is empowering.

I would be remiss if I did not address one disclaimer at the conclusion of this book. We must remember that law is a business like any other. I am a lawyer, but I am not your lawyer. It is not the intent of the author to enter into an attorney/client relationship with the reader. Nor does this book purport to supply legal advice. Finally, I do not recommend that you practice law without a license. These disclaimers are designed to place some necessary limits on what you have hopefully learned from this book.

I truly believe that if properly applied, these thinking skills can help us develop iron synapses, which will eventually build a mind of mental steel. The stronger the mind, the better the behavior. In essence, anyone can make legal philosophy work for them. Essentially, law provides the basis for a new brand of personal growth. The good news is that you don't have to graduate law school to do it.

I believe that one of the most important messages of this book is the power of advocacy. To illustrate, I will share with you a true story about my father who was also an attorney. His name was Dan Cody. My dad practiced personal injury and worker's compensation law for sixty-five years. Back in the 1960's,70's, and 80's he was known as the neighborhood lawyer. Many of our neighbors would seek his counsel on legal problems and he would never turn them down. He was a real "go to guy." He was not only their neighbor but their legal advocate as well. One such neighbor and client was Bob Moore. My father represented Bob on many legal matters over the years. He represented not only Bob, but his family members as well. Several years ago Bob Moore died of cancer.

My father and I attended his funeral. His widow approached us and told us a story about Bob's final weeks in home hospice care. One day she found Bob sitting in his chair tightly gripping something in his boney fist. She asked him what it was, but he refused to tell her. After some discussion and persuasion, he reluctantly opened his fist to reveal a scrap of paper. He gave it to his wife and she read her husband's shaky handwriting. The note read simply: DAN CODY.

Mrs. Moore reminded her husband that Dan had not represented them for years, if not decades. He replied simply: "I'm in trouble and I need my lawyer. Maybe Dan can help me one more time." What a wonderful tribute to the attorney client relationship. This story is a simple, but powerful one. It demonstrates what a legal mind can do as well as the sheer impact that advocacy can have on another human being. We can all advocate for, speak for, and defend another human being. My wish for my reader is that these legal thinking skills enable not only success in life, but someday maybe it will be your written name held tightly in a desperate, frightened fist. I truly believe that one should self-advocate first, and thereafter advocate for others.

The legal concepts provided in this book can open our eyes to a higher level of thinking. I believe we all have a grudging respect for lawyers and we have always wondered what accounts for their success. I truly hope this book has solved the mystery of legal thinking and that you can apply these fundamental legal concepts to your own life and business dealings.

The proper deployment of these simple skills can spur you on to success with great speed. The use of just a handful of these power thoughts will surely empower you. Proper thought in proper order will always attract the best in life. The law surrounds us. It permeates nearly every aspect of our lives. Law is the essence of high standards and mandates a deep knowledge of the rules of the game. If you don't know the rules, you cannot play the game. Know the rules and perform well in the courtroom of life. You don't need to be an attorney for success in life and business. Simply think like one!

About the Author

Mr Cody is a graduate of the College of St. Thomas in Saint Paul, Minnesota. He obtained his degree in sociology and graduated Magna Cum Laude. He is also a member of the Delta Epsilon Sigma Honor Society.

Brendan graduated from the William Mitchell College of Law in St. Paul, Minnesota with a Juris Doctorate. He was admitted to the Minnesota State Bar as well as Minnesota Supreme Court and the United States Supreme Court.

Brendan Cody has been advocating for his clients for over thirty years. He has argued numerous cases to administrative law judges, trial judges, juries, and appellate judges.

Brendan has been accepted as a member of the Million Dollar Advocates Forum, which is reserved exclusively for lawyers who have obtained a $1 million jury verdict. He was voted by his peers as a Super Lawyer in the year 2000 and further was selected as a member of the national Registry of Who's Who published that same year.

He thereafter began working on the curriculum that formed the foundation of *Think Like an Attorney*. Today, Mr. Cody shares his insights at events, conferences, continuing education seminars, and corporate training sessions.

Brendan has delivered keynote speeches at the following institutions: University of St. Thomas School of Law, Minnesota Paralegal Association, and Minnesota Association for Justice.

Bibliography

Ball, D. (2005) *David Ball on Damages: A Plaintiff's Attorney Guide to Personal Injury and Wrongful Death Cases* (Second Edition). Boulder Colorado: National Institute of Trial Advocacy.

Berger, G. *Ten Things I Learned from Louis Nizer*. Phillips Nizer LLP Articles

Federal Rules of Evidence (2018 Edition): Michigan Legal Publishing LTD.

Hill, N. (1937) *Think and Grow Rich*. Wise, VA: Napoleon Hill Foundation.

Minnesota Jury Instruction Guides (2018) Eagan, Minnesota: Thompson West.

Minnesota Rules of Court (2018), Eagan, Minnesota: Thompson West.

Nizer, L. (1961) *My Life in Court* (Garden City), New York: Double Day and Company Inc.

Osborn, J. J. (2003) *The Paper Chase*. Albany, New York: Whitston Publishing Company Inc.

Peale, N.V. (1956) *The Power of Positive Thinking*. New York, New York: Simon and Schuster.

Puzo, M. (1969) *The Godfather*. New York ,New York: The Penguin Group.

Turrow, S. (1977) *One L*. New York, New York: Warner Books Inc.